Series Authors
Karen Hume
Brad Ledgerwood

Series Consultants
Jennette MacKenzie, *Senior Consultant*
Damian Cooper, *Assessment*
James Coulter, *Assessment and Instruction*
Gayle Gregory, *Differentiated Instruction*
Ruth McQuirter Scott, *Word Study*

Series Writing Team
James Coulter, *Assessment*
Kathy Lazarovits, *ELL/ESL*
Liz Powell, *Instruction*
Sue Quennell, *Word Study*
Janet Lee Stinson, *Instruction*
Michael Stubitsch, *Instruction*

Subject and Specialist Reviewers
Mary Baratto, *The Arts*
Rachel Cooke, *Metacognition*
Phil Davison, *Media Literacy*
Graham Draper, *Geography*
Ian Esquivel, *Media Literacy*
Martin Gabber, *Science and Technology*
Cathy Hall, *Mathematics*
Jan Haskings-Winner, *History*
Dan Koenig, *Health*
Kathy Lazarovits, *ELL/ESL*
Janet Lee Stinson, *Media Literacy*

NELSON / EDUCATION

NELSON / EDUCATION

Nelson Literacy 7a

Director of Publishing
Kevin Martindale

Director of Publishing, Literacy
Joe Banel

Executive Managing Editor, Development
Darleen Rotozinski

Senior Product Manager
Mark Cressman

Senior Program Manager
Diane Robitaille

Developmental Editors
Gillian Scobie
Marilyn Wilson

Researcher
Catherine Rondina

Assistant Editor
Corry Codner

Bias Reviewer
Nancy Christoffer

Editorial Assistants
Adam Rennie
Kristen Sanchioni

Executive Director, Content and Media Production
Renate McCloy

Director, Content and Media Production
Carol Martin

Senior Content Production Editor
Laurie Thomas

Proofreader
Elizabeth D'Anjou

Production Manager
Helen Jager Locsin

Production Co-ordinator
Vicki Black

Director, Asset Management Services
Vicki Gould

Design Director
Ken Phipps

Managing Designer
Sasha Moroz

Series Design
Sasha Moroz

Series Wordmark
Sasha Moroz

Cover Design
Sasha Moroz
Glenn Toddun

Interior Design
Carianne Bauldry
Jarrel Breckon
Nicole Dimson
Courtney Hellam
Jennifer Laing
Eugene Lo
Sasha Moroz
Peter Papayanakis
Jan John Rivera
Carrie Scherkus
Industrial Strength

Art Buyer
Suzanne Peden

Compositor
Courtney Hellam

Photo Research and Permissions
Nicola Winstanley

Printer
Transcontinental Printing

Series Advisers and Reviewers

Gwen Babcock, Limestone DSB, ON
Jennifer Bach, Burnaby SD, BC
Karen Beamish, Peterborough, Victoria, Northumberland, and Clarington CDSB, ON
Mary Cairo, Toronto CDSB, ON
Maria Carty, Annapolis Valley Regional SB, NS
Joanna Cascioli, Hamilton-Wentworth DSB, ON
Janet Charlton, District 10, NB
Vivian Collyer, Sooke SD, BC
Anne Converset, Niagara DSB, ON
Rachel Cooke, Toronto DSB, ON
Phil Davison, Halton DSB, ON
Connie Dersch-Gunderson, Livingston Range SD, AB
Lori Driussi, Burnaby SD, BC
Judy Dunn, Kamloops/Thompson SD, BC
Eileen Eby, Greater Victoria SD, BC
Ian Esquivel, Toronto DSB, ON
Anna Filice-Gagliardi, Toronto CDSB, ON
Patty Friedrich, London DCSB, ON
Charmaine Graves, Thames Valley DSB, ON
Colleen Hayward, Toronto CDSB, ON
Irene Heffel, Edmonton SD, AB
Phyllis Hildebrandt, Lakeshore SD, MB
Brenda Lightburn, Mission SD, BC
Andrew Locker, York Region DSB, ON
Susan MacDonald, Delta SD, BC
Anne Marie McDonald, Limestone DSB, ON
Beverley May, District 2, NL
Selina Millar, Surrey SD, BC
Wanda Mills-Boone, Ottawa-Carleton DSB, ON
Lorellie Munson, York Region DSB, ON
Barb Muron, Toronto CDSB, ON
Linda O'Reilly, Educational Consultant, BC
Cathy Pollock, Toronto DSB, ON
Gina Rae, Richmond SD, BC
Sherry Skinner, Eastern SD, NL
Susan Stevens, Peel DSB, ON
Janet Lee Stinson, Simcoe County DSB, ON
Melisa Strimas, Bruce-Grey CDSB, ON
Elizabeth Stymiest, District 15, NB
Sue Taylor-Foley, South Shore Regional SB, NS
Laurie Townshend, Toronto DSB, ON
Tracy Toyama, Toronto DSB, ON
Deborah Tranton-Waghorn, Ottawa-Carleton DSB, ON
Ann Varty, Trillium Lakelands DSB, ON
Ruth Wiebe, Chilliwack SD, BC
Mark Wilderman, Saskatoon Public SD, SK
Nadia Young, Toronto CDSB, ON

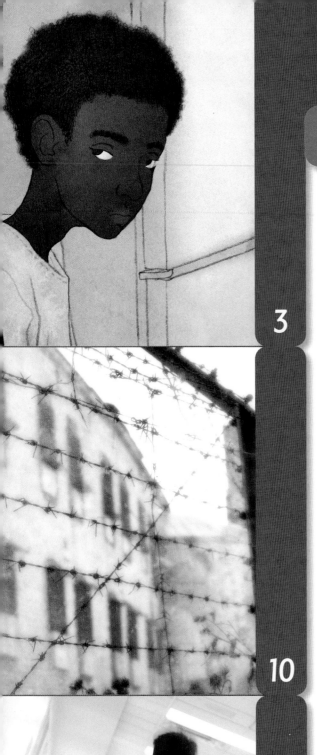

CONTENTS

Unit 1 — Step Up

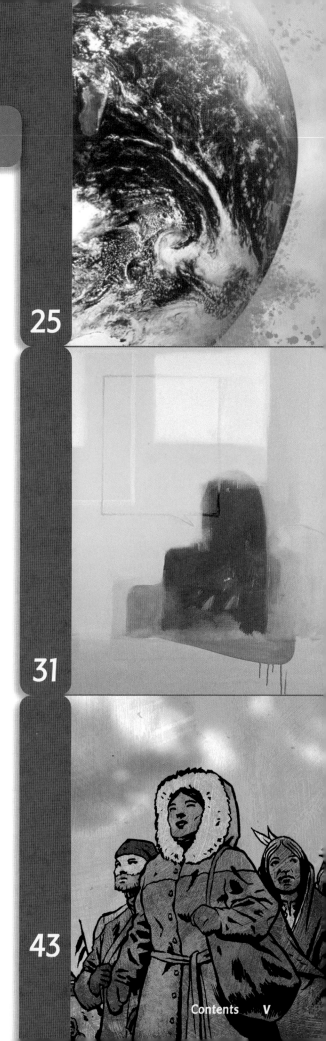

CONTENTS

Unit 2 — Tech Effects

59

63

71

78

86

104

Welcome to
Nelson Literacy

Nelson Literacy presents a rich variety of literature, informational articles, and media texts from Canada and around the world. Many of the selections offer tips to help you develop strategies in reading, oral communication, writing, and media literacy.

Here are the different kinds of pages you will see in this book:

Focus pages

These pages outline a specific strategy and describe how to use it. Included are "Transfer Your Learning" tips that show how you can apply that strategy to other strands and subjects.

Understanding Strategies

These selections have instructions in the margins that help you to understand and use reading, writing, listening, speaking, and media literacy strategies.

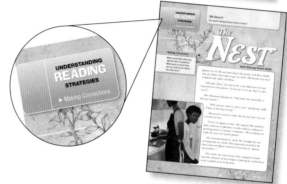

Applying Strategies

These selections give you the chance to apply the strategies you have learned. You will see a variety of formats and topics.

Transfer Your Learning

At the end of the unit, you'll have a chance to see how the strategies you have learned can help you in other subject areas such as Science and Technology, Geography, History, Health, Mathematics, and the Arts.

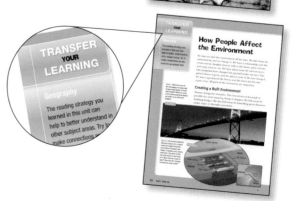

STEP UP

What inspires you to step up and take a stand?

Unit Learning Goals

- make connections while reading
- develop ideas in writing
- listen effectively
- recognize purpose and audience of media texts
- identify sequence text pattern

Transfer Your Learning: Geography

How to > Make Connections

Making connections while you read is a powerful way to make sense of new information. Making connections also helps you to respond to texts. There are three main ways to make connections.

Text-to-Self Connections

Something you're reading might remind you of an experience you've had. For example, a speech about equal rights for everyone will mean more to you if you think about a time you weren't treated fairly.

Text-to-Text Connections

One text can remind you of another text you have read or a show you have seen. For example, you read a story about a teen standing up for his beliefs and make connections to a song you've heard on the same theme.

Text-to-World Connections

Connecting to world events or issues can help you understand what you read. For example, an article about saving wildlife habitats will make more sense when you connect it to what you know about the rainforest being destroyed.

text to self

making connections

text to text

text to world

Transfer Your Learning

Across the Strands

Oral Communication: When you're listening to others talk, you make connections. If someone is telling you about a charity he volunteers for, what connection can you make to volunteer work that you have done?

Across the Curriculum

Geography: If you're studying waste management, what text-to-text connections can you make to a TV program about new methods of recycling?

Talk About It
Do adults always know what is best?

THE NEST

Short Story by Robert Zacks

Making Connections →

Make connections when you read the title of a selection. What types of connections can you make to the title of this short story?

Jimmy was 14. He was listening to his mother tell him, kindly, why she didn't want him to go on a hike. His brown eyes were clouded with sullen rebellion.

"All right, Mom," he said in the controlled voice he had learned from his parents. "If you say I can't go, then I can't, can I?"

Mrs. Swanson said gravely, "You make me sound like a dictator, Jimmy."

"Well, you are, kind of, aren't you?" said Jimmy coldly. "I have to do what you say."

His mother winced a little. She bit her lower lip and considered this.

"It isn't as simple as that," she argued. She smiled a little, however, in pleasure at such evidence of Jimmy's growing power to analyze a situation. "My decisions are made for your own good, Jimmy."

He misunderstood her smile. He thought she was treating him as a child. All his parents seemed to do these days was figure out how to hem him in. "Jimmy, you mustn't—"

The words, the restrictions, they wrapped around him like tentacles of an octopus, crushing in on his chest so he couldn't seem to breathe.

Making Connections ➜

Make text-to-self connections. Have you ever had a person in authority make a decision for you? How does thinking about that situation help you to understand how Jimmy feels?

Making Connections ➜

Make text-to-world connections as you read. What do you think of when you read the word *gang*? How does making this connection help you to understand Jimmy's mother's fear?

He was on his feet, yelling, the controlled, polite speech lost in his bursting anguish for freedom. "Everything is for my own good. Everything! But you aren't telling me the truth. You know why you don't want me to go on the hike? Because of Paul. You just don't like him."

He sucked in his breath, almost sobbing, shocked at himself and yet glad. Mrs. Swanson had an unhappy look. The Swansons were a happy family; but these days a strange restlessness had come into it.

"No," she admitted. "I don't think Paul is good for you. I don't like your associating with him."

Jimmy said, all his heart and soul in his words, "I like Paul. He's my best friend."

"His father drinks," said Mrs. Swanson quietly. "And Paul came out of reform school, didn't he? He stole from a candy store—"

"He's nice!" cried Jimmy, pain in his voice. "And he isn't a thief. He made a mistake. He told me what happened. He was showing off. And now nobody will be friends—"

"But he's formed a gang already, hasn't he? I've heard about it."

"It's just a club, that's all," said Jimmy. "And—and I'm a member. The club is running the hike."

"We won't discuss it further." Mrs. Swanson's voice was suddenly like steel. She stood up. She hesitated, pitying him, and tried to soften it with logic. "Remember, Jimmy, every time we've disagreed, it turned out I knew what I was talking about."

But he didn't listen further. Jimmy turned and blindly ran off the porch across the lawn toward the meeting place at Briggs' Drugstore.

After three blocks he slowed down, panting, his face set with fury. The habit of thinking, encouraged by his parents at every opportunity, began to function.

"'I know what's best for you. I know what's best for you.' That's all I ever hear!" muttered Jimmy.

To his reluctant mind sprang memories. The time he insisted he could swim to the raft. Mr. Swanson had curtly said no, he couldn't risk it. Jimmy had raged, with his father quietly letting him run down. Then his father had told him to go ahead, but that he'd swim next to him.

Jimmy's throat strangled suddenly at the memory—of the water constricting his windpipe dreadfully, his eyes bulging, his legs and arms numb with exhaustion from the too-long swim. And then the wonderful, strong, blessed arms of his father turning him on his back, pulling him back to shore—

It was confusing. Jimmy shook his head in bewilderment. Suddenly he felt uncertain; the rebellion drained out of him.

Paul was waiting for him at the drugstore with a stillness upon his face as he leaned against the glass front. He was about 14, with sandy hair and bright blue eyes. Jimmy saw, when he came closer, traces of tears on Paul's cheeks.

← **Making Connections**

Make connections to your own experiences as you read. We all have second thoughts about decisions we make. Notice how the author's use of a specific example helps you to connect with Jimmy's uncertainty.

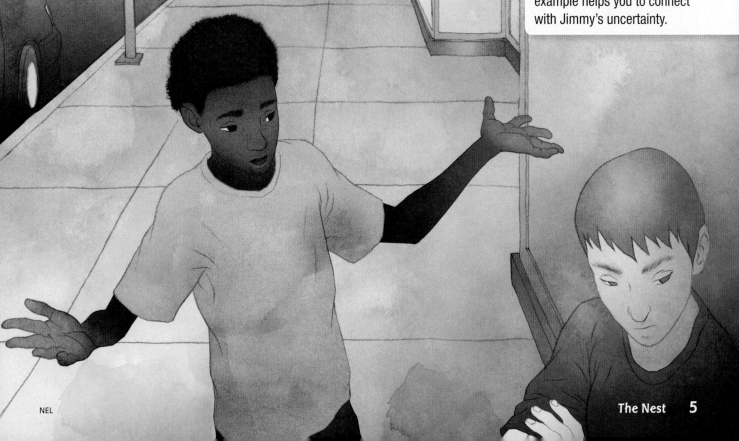

Making Connections ➜

Making connections to your own experiences can help you to form opinions about what you read. What do you think about the way that those parents reacted to Paul?

"Well," said Paul fiercely, "let's go."

Jimmy started. "Where's everybody?"

"They changed their minds," said Paul, hate in his voice.

The two boys looked at each other, and Jimmy understood. It made fury grow in him, it made him want to hit somebody. All those parents had stopped the gang from going with Paul because he was once in a reform school.

Paul said, his voice odd, "Maybe you can't go either?"

Jimmy looked deep into Paul's eyes. His heart beat fast with friendship and loyalty. "Don't be a jerk. Come on," he said cheerfully.

Paul's face changed. The hate seeped away, leaving sweetness and humbleness. He flung an arm over Jimmy's shoulder happily.

"Your—your mother doesn't care if you go, huh?" he said.

Jimmy swallowed. Paul needed this so badly. So very badly. Paul had no mother at all. And his father just didn't like looking at the world without Paul's mother, and was always drunk.

"Nah," said Jimmy. "She—she even said I should bring you to supper, afterwards. What shall I tell her, huh?"

Paul turned ashen, then flushed a deep scarlet. "Sure," he muttered. "Be glad to."

"I got to call her," said Jimmy numbly. "Just a minute."

Jimmy went into the drugstore and called his mother. He told her in a choking voice he was going on the hike, just he and Paul, and he didn't care how mad she got. "Nobody else came," he shouted into the telephone, "because all the mothers—" He was unable to go on for a moment. Then he finished. "I'm bringing him to supper afterwards, Mom. I said you asked him."

He hung up before she could answer.

They had a wonderful day. Wonderful. It was May, and the leaves on the trees were green and new. They went ten kilometres out of town. They watched chipmunks skitter. They lay on their backs and stared at fleecy white clouds changing shape. Paul's face showed his contentment. His eyes were dreamy.

Making Connections →

As you read, make text-to-text connections. How is Paul like other characters you've met in stories or shows? How does making these connections increase your understanding of Paul's character?

But Jimmy, in one cloud, saw the stern face of his mother.

But Mrs. Swanson's face, when she greeted Paul, wasn't stern at all. She looked uncertain as she studied his wistful, shy smile. Jimmy knew, of course, that his parents would wait until later to lecture him. They never made a scene before other people.

Throughout supper, Mr. Swanson was very friendly to their guest. But Jimmy could see that at the same time his father was carefully studying Paul. And Paul, never knowing, thinking they'd wanted him, had invited him, glowed and showed the side of his personality that Jimmy liked.

After they'd washed the dishes (at Paul's suggestion), Mr. Swanson nodded to Paul. "Come on, Paul," he said. "I'll show you my tool shop."

As Paul eagerly followed him down the basement steps, Mrs. Swanson touched Jimmy's shoulder. Jimmy's heart thudded as he reluctantly lingered behind. He turned and glared in defiance.

"I don't care," he whispered. "Nobody else came. I couldn't—"

"Jimmy," she said softly, and bent and kissed him. "I'm proud of you, Jimmy. You did the right thing at the right time."

"But you said—" faltered Jimmy. "I mean—"

Her eyes were very bright. "I was wrong," she said steadily. "This time I was wrong. You were right. He's a nice boy, I think."

She turned away, patting his cheek as she did so.

At first, joy filled Jimmy. Joy and pride. I'm the one who's right, he thought, dazed. My mother was wrong. Actually wrong. She admitted it.

And then came a frightening sense of loss, as well as of gain. It was like being alone, high up on a cliff where the footing was slippery with moss. Jimmy felt he had to be careful of each step. He had always been sure, even in his anger, of being able to depend on the wisdom of his father and mother. They'd always been right.

But not any more. Now they might be wrong. And Jimmy would have to decide.

Reflecting

Metacognition: How did connecting with the characters in this story help you to better understand the struggle between them?

Text-to-Self Connections: Who in the story did you connect most strongly with: Jimmy, his mother, or Paul? Explain why.

Critical Literacy: How would this story change if it were told from the mother's point of view?

Making Connections

A graphic organizer like this can help you organize the connections you made as you read this story.

Would I stand up for a friend?

connections to the story

What novels does this story remind me of?

What news items does this story remind me of?

Talk About It
In your opinion, who is responsible when a country goes to war?

Universal Soldier

Song by Buffy Sainte-Marie

He's five feet two and he's six feet four
He fights with missiles and with spears
He's all of 31 and he's only 17
He's been a soldier for a thousand years
He's a Catholic, a Hindu, an atheist, a Jain,
a Buddhist and a Baptist and a Jew
and he knows he shouldn't kill
and he knows he always will
kill you for me my friend and me for you

And he's fighting for Canada,
he's fighting for France,
he's fighting for the USA,
and he's fighting for the Russians
and he's fighting for Japan,
and he thinks we'll put an end to war this way

And he's fighting for Democracy
and fighting for the Reds
He says it's for the peace of all
He's the one who must decide
who's to live and who's to die
and he never sees the writing
on the wall

But without him how would Hitler have
condemned him at Dachau
Without him Caesar would have stood alone
He's the one who gives his body
as a weapon to a war
and without him all this killing can't go on

He's the universal soldier and he
really is to blame

His orders come from far away no more
They come from him, and you, and me
and brothers can't you see
this is not the way we put an end to war.

current anti-war poster

First They Came

Poem by Martin Niemöller

First they came for the Jews
and I did not speak out—
because I was not a Jew.

Then they came for the communists
and I did not speak out—
because I was not a communist.

Then they came for the trade unionists
and I did not speak out—
because I was not a trade unionist.

Then they came for me—
and there was no one left
to speak for me.

MEN of VALOR
They fight for you

"When last seen he was collecting Bren and Tommy Guns and preparing a defensive position which successfully covered the withdrawal from the beach."—Excerpt from citation awarding Victoria Cross to Lt.-Col. Merritt, South Saskatchewan Regt, Dieppe, Aug. 19, 1942.

World War II poster. Small print at bottom reads "Excerpt from citation awarding Victoria Cross to Lt. Col. Charles Merritt, South Saskatchewan Regt, Dieppe, Aug. 9, 1942."

Reflecting

Text-to-Text Connections: Think about this song, this poem, and the story "The Nest." What connections can you make?

Critical Thinking: Use your understanding of these connections to help you visualize a meeting of Jimmy, the universal soldier, and the "I" in the poem "First They Came." What would they all say to one another?

Talk About It

Why is it hard to stand up to powerful people?

RESISTING HITLER

Magazine Article by Susan Campbell Bartoletti

a young Helmuth Hübener

When Hitler came to power in Germany in the mid-1930s, he passed a law that required all healthy German youths to be trained "physically, intellectually, and morally." This meant that young people were required by law to join the Hitler Youth movement. Most Germans obeyed, but not all. This is the story of one teenager who didn't. His rebellion began with listening to the radio.

It was illegal at the time to listen to foreign radio broadcasts, but many Germans did. Aware that German people were listening, the British Broadcasting Corporation (BBC) broadcast the news in German. In early 1941, a soldier returning from France brought home a broken radio and gave it to Helmuth Hübener, his younger half-brother. Helmuth lived with his grandparents in Hamburg.

Sixteen-year-old Helmuth fixed the radio. After his grandparents went to bed, he toyed with the radio dials, tuning in a German-language newscast on the BBC. Night after night, Helmuth listened to the British war reports and compared them with the German news. Soon, he realized that the reports didn't add up. The Nazis, he concluded, were lying to the German people.

One night in July 1941, Helmuth invited his best friend to the apartment. "I want you to hear something," he told Karl-Heinz Schnibbe, who was 17. Karl accepted the invitation and heard the BBC for the first time. Several weeks later, another friend, 15-year-old Rudi Wobbe, joined the two boys.

One day, Helmuth decided that the German people deserved to know the truth about the Nazis. He wrote essays titled "Hitler the Murderer," "Hitler Is the Guilty One," "Do You Know They Are Lying to You?" and "Don't Believe the Nazi Party." He typed the essays and stamped each one with a swastika to look official.

Excited, Helmuth showed the bold flyers to Karl and Rudi. "Are you nuts?" said Karl, shocked. "You can't get the Nazis with these."

But Helmuth was insistent, saying, "I just want the German people to think. Don't you think everybody in Hamburg is entitled to know the truth?" Helmuth persuaded Karl and Rudi to distribute the flyers. It was dangerous work, for Nazi informers lurked everywhere and neighbours spied on neighbours.

The three boys made a pact, promising one another that if one boy got caught, he would take all the blame and not implicate the other two. Night after night, the three boys left the flyers in apartment buildings, mailboxes, phone booths, and other public places. "Once we even put one in the coat pocket of a Nazi official," said Karl.

The boys carried on their resistance activities for months. Several neighbours reported the flyers to the police, who began an investigation. On Wednesday, February 4, 1942, a suspicious co-worker told the authorities about Helmuth.

sixteen-year-old Helmuth between his two best friends, 15-year-old Rudi Wobbe (left) and 17-year-old Karl-Heinz Schnibbe (right)

police photo of Helmuth

Hamburg 346 /42

The next day, the Gestapo arrested Helmuth at work. They searched his grandparents' apartment and seized the radio, extra flyers, and a typewriter.

Three days later, Karl found out about Helmuth's arrest. "When I heard that, I felt as though I'd been hit with a club," said Karl. He agonized, worrying about Helmuth and wondering when the Gestapo would come for him and Rudi.

Meanwhile, the Gestapo beat Helmuth for two days, telling him that they knew he didn't work alone. They demanded the names of the adult ringleaders. On the second day, Helmuth broke under the torture and gave the Gestapo the names of Karl and Rudi.

The Gestapo were astonished that teenagers had conducted such resistance activity. "The Gestapo could not imagine that a 16-year-old boy could mastermind such a conspiracy," said Karl. "They wanted to find the adults behind the scenes. But there were no adults."

The Gestapo arrested Karl and Rudi. The boys were taken to Hamburg prison.

For six months, Karl, Rudi, and Helmuth were held. In August 1942, the boys were transported to Berlin for their trial. It would take place before Nazi Germany's highest court, the feared People's Court, also known as the Blood Court, since it often handed down the death sentence.

The trial was closed to the public and lasted more than six hours. The judge and the Nazi lawyer focused on Helmuth, firing question after question at him. "To this day, I'm amazed at how cool, how clear, and how smart Helmuth was," said Karl.

As Karl listened to his friend's testimony, he realized that Helmuth knew he was doomed; the People's Court intended to make an example of him. Nonetheless, Helmuth remained true to his pact, accepting full responsibility for writing and distributing the leaflets. He refused to pass on any blame to Karl and Rudi.

By taking responsibility, Helmuth saved the lives of his friends. Still, Karl received five years of hard labour for reading the leaflets, and Rudi was given ten years, because he had implicated himself more during interrogation.

The court sentenced Helmuth Hübener to death. Helmuth collapsed when he heard the sentence, but the guards yanked him to his feet. Having composed himself, Helmuth said to the court, "I haven't committed any crime. All I've done is tell the truth." Two months later, he was beheaded in Plötzensee prison in Berlin.

ANOTHER RESISTER: THE HISTORY OF JO

How hard was it to resist Hitler? Well, most people did *not* resist. In fact, some people collaborated (co-operated). Others, to protect themselves or their families, were passive (not resisting but also not helping). A very small percentage of people actually resisted Hitler.

One of those resisters was a young woman named Jannetje Johanna Schaft, known as Jo. Jo lived in the Netherlands, which Hitler invaded on May 10, 1940. To help Jewish families, Jo stole identity papers and found "safe houses." She also resisted by distributing illegal newspapers and weapons and gathering information about German military activity. More dangerously, Jo planned and completed acts of sabotage and assassination. Jo was caught by the Germans and executed in 1945.

This statue was built to honour Johanna Schaft.

Reflecting

Metacognition: What types of connections did you make most often as you read: text-to-text, text-to-self, or text-to-world? How did making connections increase your understanding of the magazine article?

Text-to-Self Connections: Imagine you were Helmuth. Would you be willing to take the same kinds of risks? Explain.

Text-to-World Connections: What connections can you make between this selection and current world events?

Talk About It
Whether they take a stand for or against something, these signs all express a point of view.

SIGNS OF THE TIMES

Signs from various sources

green is good

stand up to be counted or fall down & be forgotten

got  ?

OUR TROOPS FIGHT FOR *YOUR* SAFETY

save the

end (hate) now

I DON'T SHARE YOUR PREJUDICES

Think!.. Before it becomes illegal

PEACE
COMES WITH VICTORY

think globally act locally

standing together

united against the war
BUT not the warrior

farmers fuel cities

Reflecting

Text-to-Text Connections: Compare and contrast the messages in these signs. What other texts do these signs remind you of?

Critical Literacy: What opinions are not represented in these signs? What groups are not represented?

How to Develop Ideas

We write for many reasons. One reason is to inform our audience. This is called *expository,* or *informational, writing.* Examples of this kind of writing include newspaper articles, explanations, and research reports.

Choosing a Topic

List the topics you are interested in and want to write about. This initial list may be long and the topics very general.

Narrowing the Topic

Select one topic from your list. For example, you may have included "human rights" on your initial list. This topic is far too broad to write about. Here is one way that topic could be narrowed to a main idea or message:

human rights ⟩ citizens' rights ⟫ students' rights

Developing Subtopics

Once you have narrowed your topic, make sure you have enough details to support your main idea. Sometimes in expository writing, the details are organized into subtopics. One way to develop subtopics is to create an idea web like this one.

dress code

students' rights

attendance

classroom behaviour

Transfer Your Learning

Across the Strands

Reading: How did learning about making connections in your reading change the way you think about developing ideas for your audience?

Across the Curriculum

History: It's important to have a clear idea of your topic and to make sure that topic is not too broad. For example, if you're writing about early settlers in Canada, how might you narrow the topic?

Principals and Principles

Personal Essay by Daniel Handler

In San Francisco the weather never gets hot, and when it does it lasts only three days. On the first day, the hot weather is a surprise, and everyone wanders around carrying their sweaters. On the second day, everyone enjoys the heat. And on the third day, the cold weather returns and it is just as surprising, and everyone wanders around shivering.

One of these three-day heat waves arrived when I was in seventh grade, and on the first day everyone was grumpy because we had all dressed for fog and gloom and now had to drag our sweaters all over school. We all agreed that the next day we'd dress for warm weather, but just as the day ended, the principal made an announcement over the loudspeaker. "Students at Herbert Hoover Middle School are not allowed to wear shorts," she said, in the tone of voice she always used—a tone of voice that sounded friendly but was actually unbearably wicked.

Everyone groaned—everyone but me. "She can't do that," I said, and reached into the back of my binder. On the first day of school, we'd all received a pamphlet: "Student Rights and Responsibilities." For some reason I'd saved it, and I read one of our rights out loud: "Students have the right to free dress." I convinced everyone to wear shorts the next day in order to protest the wicked principal's unfair cancellation of one of our rights.

Developing Ideas →

When you choose a topic for a personal essay, a current experience may remind you of an experience from your past. What might have led this writer to remember an experience from Grade 7?

Developing Ideas →

Writers need to narrow their topic to focus on a single main idea. What is this writer's main idea? How does the title help you identify the main idea?

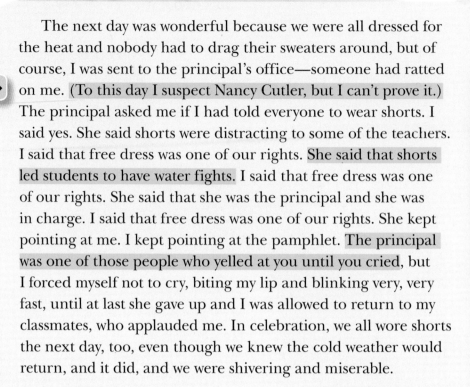

The next day was wonderful because we were all dressed for the heat and nobody had to drag their sweaters around, but of course, I was sent to the principal's office—someone had ratted on me. (To this day I suspect Nancy Cutler, but I can't prove it.) The principal asked me if I had told everyone to wear shorts. I said yes. She said shorts were distracting to some of the teachers. I said that free dress was one of our rights. She said that shorts led students to have water fights. I said that free dress was one of our rights. She said that she was the principal and she was in charge. I said that free dress was one of our rights. She kept pointing at me. I kept pointing at the pamphlet. The principal was one of those people who yelled at you until you cried, but I forced myself not to cry, biting my lip and blinking very, very fast, until at last she gave up and I was allowed to return to my classmates, who applauded me. In celebration, we all wore shorts the next day, too, even though we knew the cold weather would return, and it did, and we were shivering and miserable.

In eighth grade we got a new version of the pamphlet. Instead of "Students have the right to free dress," it read, "Students have the responsibility to dress appropriately." I threw it away.

If you stand up for your rights, you can count on the fact that the wicked people will find sneaky ways to change the rules. But you should stand up for your rights anyway, because there aren't enough sunny days in the world, and everyone should enjoy them.

Reflecting

Reading Like a Writer: This writer delivers a clear message by developing one idea: his memory of a childhood experience. Imagine you're his editor. Is there anything in this essay that you would delete to improve the message? Is there anything you would add?

Text-to-Text Connections: What stories, TV shows, or movies have you enjoyed about students taking a stand at school? How does thinking about those texts increase your understanding or appreciation of this selection?

Critical Literacy: What details in this essay make it believable? What details make it less believable?

Author Daniel Handler is better known by his pen name Lemony Snicket. He is the author of the best-selling books A Series of Unfortunate Events. *The events in this essay occurred during his adolescence in the early 1980s.*

Talk About It

What do you think it means to be a "global citizen"?

Igniting Global Change
ONE CANDLE AT A TIME

Newspaper Article by Craig Kielburger
and Marc Kielburger

Craig (left)
and Marc
Kielburger

The young woman stood alone in a silent, darkened auditorium, thousands of youth watching her as she lit a single candle that barely lit her face.

"I'm only one person. What difference can I make?" she quietly asked.

Then she turned to the four people closest to her and lit the candles they were holding. As she did that, she asked them, "I'm only one person. What difference can I make?"

Those four people walked to the corners of the room and began to light everyone's candle, including ours, asking the same humbling question over and over. Within minutes the entire auditorium was illuminated as we all chanted thunderously and in unison.

It was a moving demonstration that showed how thousands of small acts can create a tidal wave of change.

This was at an international conference we attended where youth gathered to discuss major challenges facing the world. It was full of energy, passion, and innovation, but left us a little overwhelmed. The problems we discussed were so vast that we felt like two tiny droplets of hope in a sea of despair.

Marie Abbott, of Whitehorse, Yukon, was so appalled by the news of children forced to become soldiers, she raised money for a school in Sierra Leone and a children's centre in Tanzania.

But that single flame was a symbolic gesture that reaffirmed our belief that ordinary people—students, dentists, mechanics, homemakers—can come together to make a difference. We've seen so many times that you don't have to be a prime minister to change the world, and you don't have to be rich. What you need is the courage to dream of a better tomorrow and the commitment to work with those who share your passion.

This global togetherness is what drives today's generation of young social activists. Every day we meet incredible youth who are devoted to issues such as ending poverty, fighting AIDS, and protecting the environment. They are politically aware and dedicated to making a difference.

Their idealism is grounded in a new reality. The personal computer—which celebrated its 25th birthday in August—and the resulting Internet boom are connecting young people to all corners of the globe.

With the click of a mouse, a 12-year-old in Toronto can now learn about how child labour endangers children in India, or how AIDS affects northern Malawi. With another click of the mouse, that child can contact other people around the world who are interested in the same issues.

And not only can they see the world through the Internet, but the ease of international travel means that young people can also experience the world first-hand. Africa, or anywhere else, is no longer a far-off place.

Today's youth are the first generation of global citizens.

As technology continues to break down borders, young people are the ones who readily embrace it because they've had it all their lives. While previous generations grew up with global divisions such as the Berlin Wall, this one is surrounded by the tools to unify us.

Armed with this new global perspective, youth are challenging their peers and their governments on global issues. They are becoming responsible, engaged citizens.

A recent youth opinion poll found that more than 80% of young Canadians are concerned about global issues such as AIDS, human rights, and poverty. Two-thirds of them said they use the Internet to research these issues.

Like our friend Fiona who, after learning about famine in Niger, e-mailed everyone she knew asking who wanted to help make a difference. Together, she and her friends started Oakville Teenagers in Action. In less than a year they raised enough money to build a school in Sierra Leone and send local teens on volunteer trips to Africa.

When tragedy hit her small community, Stephanie Subject of Killarney, British Columbia, took action. She started an organization, called Youth in Action to help at-risk teenagers.

Young people like this are at the forefront of a movement toward global consciousness that will have huge political and social implications. Because the world is more interconnected than at any time in history, they are more likely to vote with international issues in mind, do business with other countries, learn a foreign language, and even live or work abroad.

With youth at the helm, this new kind of globalization will focus not just on economics and technology, but also on human rights and environmental protection. Its impact has the potential to be far greater than we can even imagine.

Change is already starting to happen. After years of public pressure, leaders of the world's richest nations pledged in 2005 to double aid to Africa and cut billions of dollars in debt owed by poor countries. Much of that pressure came from youth who, with their increased understanding of poverty and ability to organize online, fought for change.

Even everyday local actions reflect this new reality. Whether it's through shopping for fair-trade clothing, signing an online petition, or corresponding with someone in a different country, young people are using their new-found worldliness to make a statement.

And like that flame, together they can make a difference.

Craig Kielburger founded the charitable organization Free the Children when he was 12, more than 10 years ago. Both he and his brother Marc are very active in the Free the Children organization. The brothers are passionate about activism and social involvement. Through public speaking and writing, they tell others about the need for action. Free the Children helps children around the world, by providing education and programs that help them help themselves.

Reflecting

Reading Like a Writer: The authors use supporting details to convince you that individuals acting together can create positive change. Which details do you find most persuasive?

Making Connections: What connections did you make as you read this article? How did making those connections help you to understand the article?

Critical Literacy: What do Craig and Marc hope to achieve with this article? Is the article effective? Why or why not?

Talk About It

What does the expression "if the world were a village" mean to you?

Welcome to the Global Village

**Nonfiction Article by
David J. Smith, adapted from
*If the World Were a Village***

The following selection appeared originally in a book created to help students understand some pretty mind-boggling numbers and startling statistics. In early 2007, there were over 6 600 000 000 (6 billion 600 million) people on Earth!

Numbers this big are hard to understand, but what if we imagined the whole population of the world as a village of just 100 people? Come and meet the people of the global village.

FOOD

There is no shortage of food in the global village. If all the food were divided equally, everyone would have enough to eat. But the food isn't divided equally. So although there is enough to feed the villagers, not everyone is well fed:

- 50 people do not have a reliable source of food and are hungry some or all of the time.

- 20 other people are severely undernourished.

- Only 30 people always have enough to eat.

Food Distribution in the Global Village

30 people always have enough to eat

50 people do not have a reliable source of food and are hungry some or all of the time

20 other people are severely undernourished

MONEY AND POSSESSIONS

In one part of the village, someone buys a new car. In another, a man repairs a bicycle, his family's most valued possession. If all the money in the village were divided equally, each person would have about $6200 per year. But in the global village, money isn't divided equally.

- The richest 20 people each have more than $9000 a year.

- The poorest 20 people each have less than $1 a day.

- The other 60 people have something in between.

The average cost of food, shelter, and other necessities in the village is $4000 to $5000 per year. Many people don't have enough money to meet these basic needs.

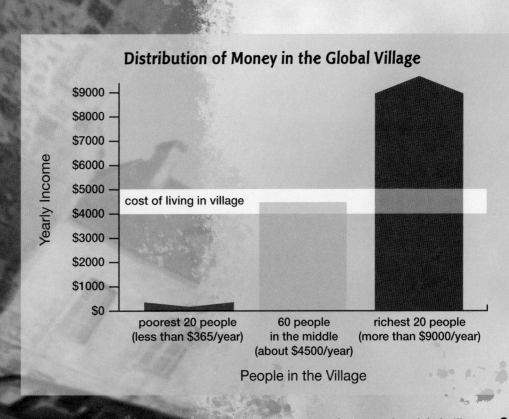

Distribution of Money in the Global Village

Yearly Income

$9000
$8000
$7000
$6000
$5000
$4000
$3000
$2000
$1000
$0

cost of living in village

poorest 20 people
(less than $365/year)

60 people
in the middle
(about $4500/year)

richest 20 people
(more than $9000/year)

People in the Village

AIR AND WATER

In most of the village, the air is healthy and the water is clean. But for some villagers, the air and water are soured by pollution, putting them at risk for diseases. And in places, water is in short supply. Instead of turning on a tap, some villagers must walk long distances to find clean water.

How many people in the village of 100 have clean air, a nearby source of clean water, and access to adequate sanitation?

CLEAN AIR

- 68 breathe clean air.

- 32 breathe air that is unhealthy because of pollution.

CLEAN WATER

- 75 have access to a source of safe water either in their homes or within a short distance.

- 25 do not and must spend a large part of each day simply getting safe water (most of the work collecting water is done by women and girls).

SANITATION AND SEWAGE

- 60 have access to adequate sanitation—they have public or household sewage disposal.

- 40 do not.

Clean Water Distribution in the Global Village

75 people have safe water

25 people do not have safe water in their homes or close by

In this village, how many people work to help others? Is it as few as one? Volunteers, government agencies, and aid are desperately needed in this village—to help with providing adequate food, energy, shelter, and literacy for all. Understanding the other people who live in our village—our world—is an important first step in becoming a global citizen.

Reflecting

Reading Like a Writer: This author decided to represent the world population as a village of 100 people. How did that decision help you to understand the problems we face?

Metacognition: How did the charts help you to understand the concepts in each section?

Text-to-Self Connection: What group do you connect with in this selection? How does where you live in the world influence that connection?

How to → Listen Effectively

To listen effectively you need to *pay attention* to how something is said, as well as what is said. You have to *participate* in the conversation—even though you may not *say* anything.

Here are some simple things good listeners do:

- **Make connections.** Think about how what the speaker says connects to your own experiences.

- **Ask relevant questions.** For example, "What do you mean when you say …?", "Is that like …?"

- **Repeat or summarize what you hear.** For example, "So, you're saying you need support for your fundraiser. Tell me exactly how I can help."

- **Identify point of view.** Listen for clues that help you identify the speaker's views or opinions.

- **Show you understand (or don't) by the expression on your face.** Facial expressions (frowning, smiling, looking confused) can be as effective as saying something. Also, your facial expressions help prepare the speaker for your verbal response.

Good Listening Practices in Action

ALISON: Paul, can you help with our marathon this weekend?

PAUL: This weekend? I think so.

ALISON: It's only for an hour on Sunday.

PAUL: What exactly can I do?

ALISON: We need someone to register runners and accept completed donation forms.

PAUL: Just like the marathon last year. You need me to help for an hour with registering runners. I'd be glad to help.

Transfer Your Learning

Across the Strands

Reading: Which of the above listening strategies might be helpful when you are reading?

Across the Curriculum

Science: These listening practices are effective in every subject area. For example, if you're listening to a classmate's presentation on ecosystems, which practices would you use to better understand what is said?

Talk About It

Why do we sometimes look for others to blame?

Script by Simon Parke

Listening Effectively →

An important aspect of good listening is asking questions. What examples of good listening can you find in this script?

(The two Mels stand side by side.)

MEL 1:	Know what, Mel?
MEL 2:	What's that, Mel?
MEL 1:	It's a mess, Mel.
MEL 2:	What's a mess, Mel?
MEL 1:	This country, Mel.
MEL 2:	Oh yeah—this country's a mess, and no mistake.
MEL 1:	Very true.
MEL 2:	That we can say.
MEL 1:	Yep.
MEL 2:	With no dispute.
MEL 1:	Nope.
MEL 2:	This country is a mess.
MEL 1:	Right.
MEL 2:	Right.
MEL 1:	Right. So … er ….
MEL 2:	So what?
MEL 1:	So who can we blame?
MEL 2:	How d'you mean?
MEL 1:	Who can we blame?
MEL 2:	Blame?
MEL 1:	Blame! For the mess!
MEL 2:	Oh yeah—the mess.

MEL 1: We've got to blame someone.

MEL 2: True.

MEL 1: Cos I'm not taking the blame.

MEL 2: Oh.

MEL 1: Well are you taking the blame?

MEL 2: Oh no Mel—I'm not taking the blame.

MEL 1: No—I didn't think so. So who is?

MEL 2: Who is what?

MEL 1: Taking the blame!

MEL 2: Oh yeah—taking the blame. *(Pause)* Well, I don't know—we could ask Gary if he would.

MEL 1: Gary's a friend.

MEL 2: Well how about your dad?

MEL 1: You can't ask family.

MEL 2: Bit difficult then cos if you can't choose friends or family, that just leaves all those we don't know— you know, people who are different from us. And I mean, we can hardly blame them, can we?

MEL 1: Why not?

MEL 2: *(Pause)* Well—

MEL 1: They sound pretty ideal to me—

MEL 2: *(Pause)* But—

MEL 1: I mean, we blame them cos they are different.

MEL 2: Do you think so?

MEL 1: Well, why should they be different? What's wrong with us and the way we do things?

Listening Effectively →

Listening carefully can give you clues to a speaker's point of view. As you read, think about the points of view in Mel 1 and Mel 2's conversation.

MEL 2: Nothing at all.

MEL 1: Think they know it all, do they?

MEL 2: Think they know better than us?

MEL 1: They look different.

MEL 2: Dress different.

MEL 1: Cook different.

MEL 2: Think different.

MEL 1: Act different—I mean, what's their game? No wonder this country's in a mess! Do you know who I blame?

MEL 2: Who?

MEL 1: Everyone who's different!

(The following section involves increasing pace, frenzied pointing, and a crescendo of noise.)

MEL 1: I blame them—and them—and them—

MEL 2: And them—and them—and them—

M AND M: *(Alternately, then merging)* And them—and them—and them— and them—and them *(etc. etc.)*

(Stillness)

MEL 1: Makes you feel better, doesn't it?

MEL 2: What?

MEL 1: Passing the blame.

← Listening Effectively

Effective listeners identify the speaker's point of view. By the end of this selection, have Mel 1 and Mel 2 understood each other's point of view? How can you tell?

Reflecting

Metacognition: Think about how this script is similar to or different from conversations you've had. What could you learn from this script about effective listening strategies? What could you teach Mel 1 and Mel 2 about effective listening strategies?

Critical Thinking: Why would the author have given the only two characters the same name?

Text-to-Text Connections: What text-to-text connections can you make between this script and the poem "First They Came"?

THE TIGER WHO WOULD BE KING

Fable by James Thurber

One morning the tiger woke up in the jungle and told his mate that he was king of beasts.

"Leo, the lion, is king of beasts," she said.

"We need a change," said the tiger. "The creatures are crying for a change."

The tigress listened but she could hear no crying, except that of her cubs.

"I'll be king of beasts by the time the moon rises," said the tiger. "It will be a yellow moon with black stripes, in my honour."

"Oh, sure," said the tigress as she went to look after her young, one of whom, a male, very like his father, had got an imaginary thorn in his paw.

The tiger prowled through the jungle till he came to the lion's den. "Come out," he roared, "and greet the king of beasts! The king is dead, long live the king!"

Inside the den, the lioness woke her mate. "The king is here to see you," she said.

"What king?" he inquired, sleepily.

"The king of beasts," she said.

"I am the king of beasts," roared Leo, and he charged out of the den to defend his crown against the pretender.

It was a terrible fight, and it lasted until the setting of the sun. All the animals of the jungle joined in, some taking the side of the tiger and others the side of the lion. Every creature from the aardvark to the zebra took part in the struggle to overthrow the lion or to repulse the tiger, and some did not know which they were fighting for, and some fought for both, and some fought whoever was nearest, and some fought for the sake of fighting.

"What are we fighting for?" someone asked the aardvark.

"The old order," said the aardvark.

"What are we dying for?" someone asked the zebra.

"The new order," said the zebra.

When the moon rose it shone upon a jungle in which nothing stirred except a macaw and a cockatoo, screaming in horror. All the beasts were dead except the tiger, and his days were numbered and his time was ticking away. He was monarch of all he surveyed, but it didn't seem to mean anything.

Moral: You can't very well be king of beasts if there aren't any.

James Thurber (1894–1961) was born in Columbus, Ohio. He was known for his simple, witty short stories and cartoons dealing with the frustrations of modern life.

Reflecting

Listening Effectively: Fables were originally told aloud. If you were listening to this fable, at what points would you show that you understood it?

Text-to-World Connections: How does your background knowledge of the animal kingdom help you to understand this struggle for power?

How to ➤ # Recognize Purpose and Audience

We enjoy media when we watch TV, surf the net, listen to the radio, or look at an ad in a favourite magazine. As "consumers" of media texts, we need to remember that all media texts are carefully planned and constructed to have a specific effect on their intended audience.

A TV news story about a local school sporting event may seem to be very straightforward but the news station had to choose who to film, who to interview, and what information to report. All of these choices will determine what the message of the news story is and what audience that message will appeal to. Different viewers will feel very differently about what was included and the choices made by the camera operator, reporter, editor, and producer.

Some Questions to Ask about Media Texts

Purpose

• Who created the media text?

• Who benefits from the media text? For example, if the media text is trying to sell you something, then private interests (companies) benefit from the text. If the media text is meant to inform the public (for example, an ad to encourage people to stop smoking), then the public benefits from the text.

• Why was the media text created? What is the purpose or intention of the media text? It can be to inform, entertain, or persuade. For example, an ad for a movie is trying to persuade you to do something very specific: watch that movie.

I.D.

orca soundings

Vicki Grant

book cover

book cover

THAT THING YOU FALL INTO

~ BY DIANA TAMBLYN ~

zine cover

Audience

- What audience is the media text intended for? How do you know? What specific features of the media text (music, colours, text, mood, and so on) appeal to such an audience? For example, a media text produced to appeal to teens might include young actors and use modern music.

- How might different audiences interpret the media text? For example, a teenager's response would differ from a parent's response.

- How would you change the media text to appeal to a different audience or to tell another side of the story? For example, an informational text could be changed into a graphic story to appeal to a different audience.

newspaper

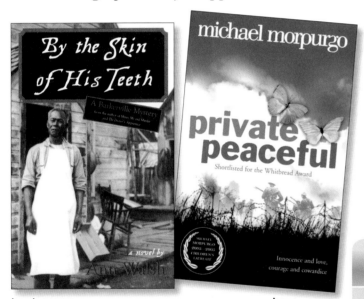

book cover   book cover

comic strip

Transfer Your Learning

Across the Strands

Oral Communication: When you're listening to oral texts you can ask these same questions. You will be a much more effective listener if you think about how speakers craft their messages to appeal to particular audiences. Think of a radio ad you have recently heard. What was the purpose and who was the intended audience?

Across the Curriculum

The Arts: When you view a painting or listen to music, you can use these same questions. Think of a song you've heard recently. What is its purpose and who is its intended audience?

Talk About It

Why do comic strips appeal to so many people?

RELEASE THE CRICKETS!

Comic Strips by Jerry Scott and Jim Borgman, creators of *Zits*

Recognizing Purpose and Audience

The purpose of most comic strips is to entertain. As you read, think about whether that's the only purpose of this series of comic strips.

Reflecting

Metacognition: What strategies do you use to help you recognize purpose and audience?

Critical Literacy: What attitude do the creators of *Zits* want you to have toward the adults in these strips? What attitude do the creators want you to have toward the teenagers? What clues in these strips reveal this attitude?

Connecting to Other Media: How does the portrayal of teenagers here compare to the portrayal of teenagers in any movies you've recently seen?

Talk About It
Does a good song always have a message?

I NEED TO WAKE UP

Song by Melissa Etheridge

The documentary *An Inconvenient Truth* was an award-winning and popular movie about the issue of global warming. Songwriter Melissa Etheridge wrote the song "I Need to Wake Up" for this movie.

Have I been sleeping?
I've been so still
Afraid of crumbling
Have I been careless?
Dismissing all the distant rumblings
Take me where I am supposed to be
To comprehend the things that I can't see

(Chorus)
Cause I need to move
I need to wake up
I need to change
I need to shake up
I need to speak out
Something's got to break up
I've been asleep
And I need to wake up
Now

And as a child
I danced like it was 1999
My dreams were wild
The promise of this new world
Would be mine
Now I am throwing off the carelessness of youth
To listen to an inconvenient truth

That I need to move … *(repeat chorus)*

I am not an island
I am not alone
I am my intentions
Trapped here in this flesh and bone

And I need to move … *(repeat chorus)*

I want to change
I need to shake up
I need to speak out
Oh, something's got to break up
I've been asleep
And I need to wake up
Now

Reflecting

Metacognition: How does knowing why the song was written increase your understanding of, or appreciation for, this song?

Connecting to Other Media: Think about other movies you've watched and their sound tracks. What do you think directors have to consider when choosing music to go with a movie?

Sequence

Expository, or *informational,* text uses a wide variety of patterns. When you recognize the pattern, it's easier to understand the text. One very common pattern is sequence. Dictionaries and manuals are sequenced: *bat* follows *apple.*

Selections using a sequence text pattern may have information listed in order of importance or in the order that something happens. The following examples show two ways that sequence texts can be organized.

When the information is listed in order of importance, it is often numbered. When the information is given in the order that something happened, it often includes dates.

Reasons to Stop Global Warming

1. Protect the environment

2. Prevent drastic climate change

3. Stop glaciers from melting

4. Slow the over-consumption of limited resources

This sequence shows order of importance, from most important to least important.

Light-Bulb Invention Timeline

regular light bulb	fluorescent light bulb	compact fluorescent light bulb
1906	1936	1970s

This sequence shows the order that the events happened.

Key words that signal a sequence text pattern include:
first, second, third
to begin, next, finally
most important, also

Transfer Your Learning

Across the Strands

Writing: In your own writing, when would it be most helpful to use a sequence text pattern?

Across the Curriculum

Science: When you follow the steps in an experiment, you are following sequence text pattern. What do you think might happen if the steps were not in order?

Sequence Text Pattern

History texts often follow a time sequence pattern. What words or phrases in this graphic text suggest time order?

Talk About It

What might be an obstacle to peace between two groups?

The Girl Who Called for Peace

Graphic Nonfiction by Ho Che Anderson

IT'S THE EARLY 1700S IN THE HUDSON BAY AREA. THE CREE AND CHIPEWYAN DENE PEOPLE ARE AT WAR. THE CREE HAVE JUST RAIDED THE VILLAGE OF A YOUNG CHIPEWYAN WOMAN, THANADELTHUR.

MY FAMILY ARE ALL GONE! I'VE BEEN CAPTURED BY THE CREE.

DURING HER TIME WITH THE CREE, THANADELTHUR LEARNS THEIR LANGUAGE.

YOU CLUMSY GIRL, DROP TONIGHT'S DINNER AND YOU DON'T EAT!

WE HAVE TO KEEP MOVING!

DURING THE WINTER, THANADELTHUR AND ANOTHER CHIPEWYAN WOMAN ESCAPE.

THANADELTHUR SURVIVES THE HARSH JOURNEY ACROSS THE BARRENS, BUT HER FRIEND DOES NOT. IN LATE 1714, THANADELTHUR ARRIVES AT FORT YORK—A TRADING POST FOR THE HUDSON'S BAY COMPANY.

GET HER INSIDE WHERE IT'S WARM.

AT THE FORT, THANADELTHUR SEES CREE HUNTERS TRADE FURS FOR ITEMS THAT HER PEOPLE ALSO NEED. SHE MEETS JAMES KNIGHT, THE GOVERNOR OF FORT YORK.

Sequence Text Pattern

Sequence text pattern often highlights important events. How has this pattern helped to emphasize the significance of Thanadelthur meeting the governor?

JAMES KNIGHT WANTS PEACE BETWEEN THE CREE AND CHIPEWYAN PEOPLES.

STOP THE WAR AND WE'LL TRADE WITH BOTH PEOPLES.

IN THE SPRING OF 1715, THANADELTHUR AND JAMES DISCUSS A PLAN FOR PEACE.

WE MUST HAVE PEACE SO THAT MY PEOPLE CAN ALSO TRADE WITH YOU.

ON JUNE 27, 1715, THANADELTHUR LEAVES FORT YORK WITH A PEACE DELEGATION: A GROUP OF 150 CREE PEOPLE AND ENGLISHMAN WILLIAM STUART. THEY TRAVEL TOWARD HER PEOPLE.

MY PEOPLE WILL BE PLEASED WHEN THEY HEAR A NEW FORT WILL BE BUILT NEAR THEM.

The Girl Who Called for Peace

Talk About It
Can small acts have world-wide impact?

The Birdman

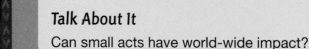

Picture Book by Veronika Martinova Charles, Annouchka Gravel Galouchko, and Stéphan Daigle

Noor Nobi lived in the big, bustling city of Calcutta. In the little laneways among the crumbling houses, the air hung heavy with heat and hummed with the sound of sewing machines.

The sun-scorched ground was littered with mango pits, melon rinds, blackened banana peels—and with scraps of colourful fabric and thread.

Many tailors worked there. Just like his father and grandfather, Noor Nobi laboured every day, sewing baby clothes.

First he pulled a piece of fabric from the stack. He carefully measured it, marked it with chalk, and cut it to the size of a brown paper pattern. Then he sewed a tiny dress with neat rows of stitches, adding a collar and ribbons and ruffles.

Sometimes while he sewed, birds waited for bits of thread. Noor Nobi made sure to drop a few scraps now and then so they could weave them into their nests. Noor Nobi enjoyed his work, but more than anything, he loved his three children.

Seven days a week, from dawn to dusk, Noor Nobi worked to feed his little ones and to keep a roof over their heads. He was working when the accident happened—the accident that took them from him forever.

For many weeks after that, the sewing machine stood silent. Even the birds stayed away. Noor Nobi was overwhelmed with grief. He sat alone, staring at the walls, unable even to cry. Just as the rain refused to relieve the parched earth, no tears would come to wash away Noor Nobi's despair.

Then one day, Noor Nobi went outside. The thick heat wrapped itself around him, but he didn't feel it. He wandered aimlessly through the hot, thirsty city.

The road was filled with cars, buses, wheelbarrows, animals, and rickshaws, all trying to avoid each other. There was honking and squealing everywhere, but Noor Nobi was blind and deaf to it.

Hours later, Noor Nobi found himself in a large market. Nothing—not the tables heaped with fruits, vegetables, and spices, not the pots and clothes that hung everywhere—caught his eye. But when he came to cages and cages crammed with birds, Noor Nobi saw those.

"Poor creatures! Once they were free and now they are miserable," he thought. "Life is so precious and fragile. In an instant it can change or be snatched away." For the first time in days, Noor Nobi allowed himself to think of his children.

"No magic can bring my little ones back," Noor Nobi admitted, "but maybe I can help these small creatures and relieve them of their pain." Noor Nobi reached deep into his pocket and found almost nothing there.

He watched as people bought the birds and carried them away. Finally, only one remained. "How much for that bird?" Noor Nobi asked the vendor.

"Whatever you can pay," the man replied. "I'm closing now."

Noor Nobi bought the bird and carried it through the dusty laneways, past the houses, until he came to an open space.

There, in the shade of a big banyan tree, Noor Nobi took the bird out of its cage. The trembling creature spread its wings and fluttered into the air.

Noor Nobi watched the bird fly to its freedom and thought of his children. This time, the emptiness in his heart filled a bit.

"Next week, I'll buy more birds," Noor Nobi decided. He returned to his machine and sewed dresses late into the night. For six more days, he worked harder than he had ever worked before.

On Monday morning, the coins, heavy in Noor Nobi's pocket, jingled as he walked to the market.

Noor Nobi waited in the sweltering heat until noon, when the prices of unsold birds dropped. Only the small, sickly ones were left. This time, he bargained for as many birds as he could buy.

At home, he poured water into a bowl for the birds to drink and sprinkled grain on the ground for them to eat. He nursed them back to health, and when they were well and strong, he took them to the big banyan tree.

One at a time, Noor Nobi scooped them up and caressed their feathers. "Fly, Little One!" he whispered, as he released each bird in turn.

Timidly at first, the birds flapped their wings. Then they rose through the branches toward the open sky. Noor Nobi's heart soared with them.

As he watched, a few drops of water trickled down his face. Soon more poured down upon him. As Noor Nobi wept, the scorched, dry earth finally got relief. The monsoon rains had begun.

Noor Nobi is still a tailor for six days a week. But every seventh day—on Mondays—he is someone quite remarkable. On Mondays, Noor Nobi is the Birdman.

People come each week to watch what happens under the banyan tree. Some smile behind their hands, some say the Birdman is crazy, some stand respectfully, and some think nothing at all. But most forget their troubles, just for a moment, each time a bird takes flight.

Today the hum of sewing machines in the little laneways has been joined by the songs of thousands of freed birds.

And each week their songs grow louder.

The Story Behind This Story

In the following article, author Veronika Martinova Charles explains why she wrote The Birdman.

On a dreary November day not so long ago, an article appeared in *The Toronto Star*. The headline read "The 'Birdman of Calcutta' frees his flock." The story told of a man who had made it his mission—one rooted in personal tragedy—to free countless caged birds.

Perhaps it was because I have a fascination with bird imagery. Perhaps it was because the man was a tailor, and I had spent many childhood hours playing games with buttons and fabric scraps beside my mother's sewing machine. Whatever the reason, I couldn't get the article out of my mind. I had to know more about this "Birdman." I called the newspaper and asked if they could put me in touch with the journalist who had written the story. The next morning my telephone rang.

"This is Azizur Rahman," said a voice over a crackling telephone line. "I'm calling from India. If you want to meet the Birdman, visit Calcutta and I'll introduce you to him myself. But if you are coming, you should do it before the monsoon season starts." I knew right then that if I didn't go, I would always regret it.

As I landed in Calcutta after 26 long hours of travel, I was not the only one wondering what on earth I was doing. Azizur was waiting for me with a shy and bewildered Birdman.

Noor Nobi

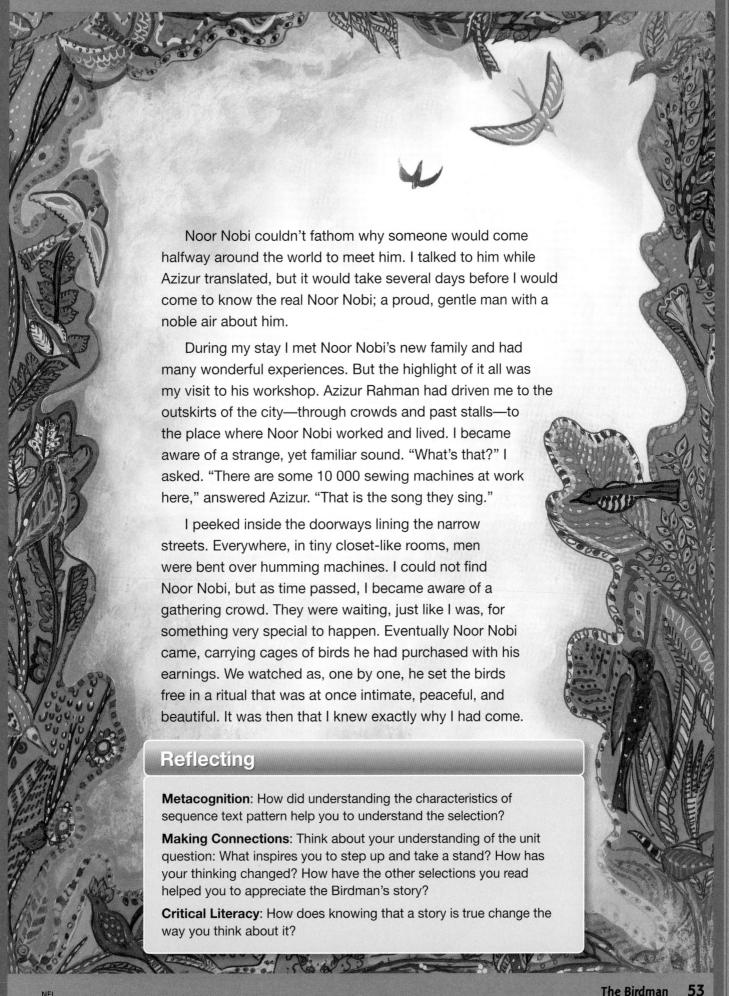

Noor Nobi couldn't fathom why someone would come halfway around the world to meet him. I talked to him while Azizur translated, but it would take several days before I would come to know the real Noor Nobi; a proud, gentle man with a noble air about him.

During my stay I met Noor Nobi's new family and had many wonderful experiences. But the highlight of it all was my visit to his workshop. Azizur Rahman had driven me to the outskirts of the city—through crowds and past stalls—to the place where Noor Nobi worked and lived. I became aware of a strange, yet familiar sound. "What's that?" I asked. "There are some 10 000 sewing machines at work here," answered Azizur. "That is the song they sing."

I peeked inside the doorways lining the narrow streets. Everywhere, in tiny closet-like rooms, men were bent over humming machines. I could not find Noor Nobi, but as time passed, I became aware of a gathering crowd. They were waiting, just like I was, for something very special to happen. Eventually Noor Nobi came, carrying cages of birds he had purchased with his earnings. We watched as, one by one, he set the birds free in a ritual that was at once intimate, peaceful, and beautiful. It was then that I knew exactly why I had come.

Reflecting

Metacognition: How did understanding the characteristics of sequence text pattern help you to understand the selection?

Making Connections: Think about your understanding of the unit question: What inspires you to step up and take a stand? How has your thinking changed? How have the other selections you read helped you to appreciate the Birdman's story?

Critical Literacy: How does knowing that a story is true change the way you think about it?

TRANSFER YOUR LEARNING

Geography

The reading strategy you learned in this unit can help you to better understand text in other subject areas. Try to make connections as you read this geography text.

How People Affect the Environment

We interact with the environment all the time. We take from the environment, and we change it. We have a relationship with the environment. Imagine that we walk in the forest, pick a flower, and enjoy what we see. We have taken from the environment. Our footprints have changed the ground under our feet. The picked flower is gone, and the plant's cycle of life has changed. We have experienced the forest, and the forest has become a part of us. All parts of the interaction are important.

Creating a Built Environment

Human beings are inventive. This inventiveness has made it possible for many amazing things to happen. We link areas by building bridges. We also link areas by tunnelling great distances under water or through mountains.

Figure 1: What are some of the advantages to being able to span huge bodies of water with bridges? What are some of the environmental problems we could cause with such bridges?

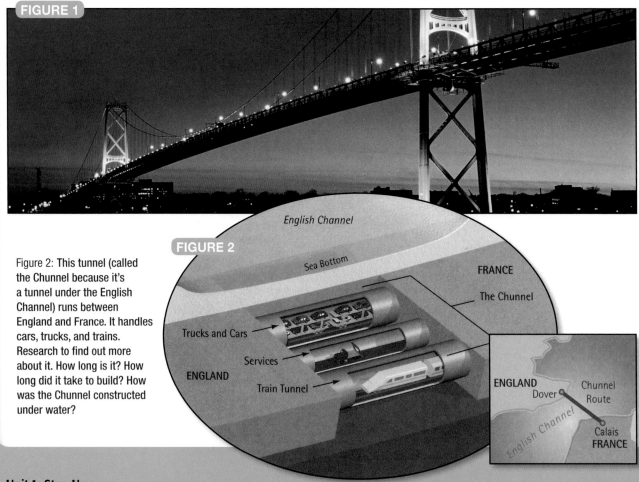

FIGURE 1

FIGURE 2

English Channel

Sea Bottom

FRANCE

The Chunnel

Trucks and Cars

Services

ENGLAND

Train Tunnel

ENGLAND
Dover

Chunnel Route

English Channel

Calais
FRANCE

Figure 2: This tunnel (called the Chunnel because it's a tunnel under the English Channel) runs between England and France. It handles cars, trucks, and trains. Research to find out more about it. How long is it? How long did it take to build? How was the Chunnel constructed under water?

We control our local environments through engineering and technology. We add heat or cold to our buildings and homes when we need it. We use resources such as oil, natural gas, and coal to produce electricity. We have learned to take advantage of the sun, moving water, the tides, and the wind to provide power.

Big urban areas use up a lot of energy. We have built power lines to move energy to cities and towns from the power sources.

Figure 3: **A windmill farm can provide enough energy to meet the needs of a town of 50 000. Could every community have one of these?**

Figure 4: **The power in these lines was generated from three major source types. Can you name them?**

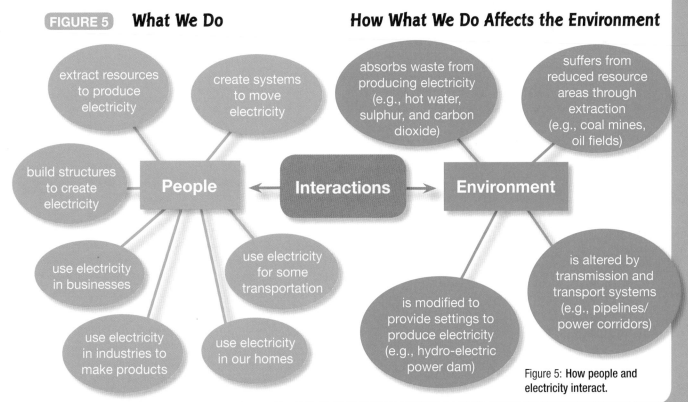

What We Do

- extract resources to produce electricity
- create systems to move electricity
- build structures to create electricity
- use electricity in businesses
- use electricity for some transportation
- use electricity in industries to make products
- use electricity in our homes

People ← **Interactions** → **Environment**

How What We Do Affects the Environment

- absorbs waste from producing electricity (e.g., hot water, sulphur, and carbon dioxide)
- suffers from reduced resource areas through extraction (e.g., coal mines, oil fields)
- is modified to provide settings to produce electricity (e.g., hydro-electric power dam)
- is altered by transmission and transport systems (e.g., pipelines/power corridors)

Figure 5: **How people and electricity interact.**

Waste Management

The artificial environments in our cities waste a lot of energy. In recent years, we have tried to use more energy-saving methods such as better insulation, windows, heating systems, and lighting. In spite of this, Canada is a world leader in energy consumption. This is not a "Number 1" that we want. We can all reduce the amount of electricity we use. Just remembering to turn off the lights would help a lot!

FIGURE 6

Figure 6: **What is your opinion about what we should do with all the garbage we produce?**

Put the Garbage Out

When we use resources, we also generate waste products—leftover, unwanted resources. Some societies generate very little waste of this kind. Others, like ours, create huge amounts. North America has a major problem storing and disposing of its waste products.

FIGURE 7

Who Produces the Most Garbage?
kg/person/day

Canada	1.7
Australia	1.6
United States	1.6
Switzerland	1.3
Netherlands	1.1
United Kingdom	0.9
Japan	0.9
Sweden	0.8
China	0.5

Family of 4 in 1 Year

2400 kg

500 kg

Recycles   Throws out as garbage

Sweden produces less than half the garbage per person that Canada does. Why do you think Canada produces the most garbage per person?

Figure 7: **Compare how much garbage we trash to how much we recycle.**

Reflecting

Metacognition: How did making connections as you read help you understand this text? What types of connections (text-to-text, text-to-self, text-to-world) were most helpful? What other strategies from the unit helped you understand this text?

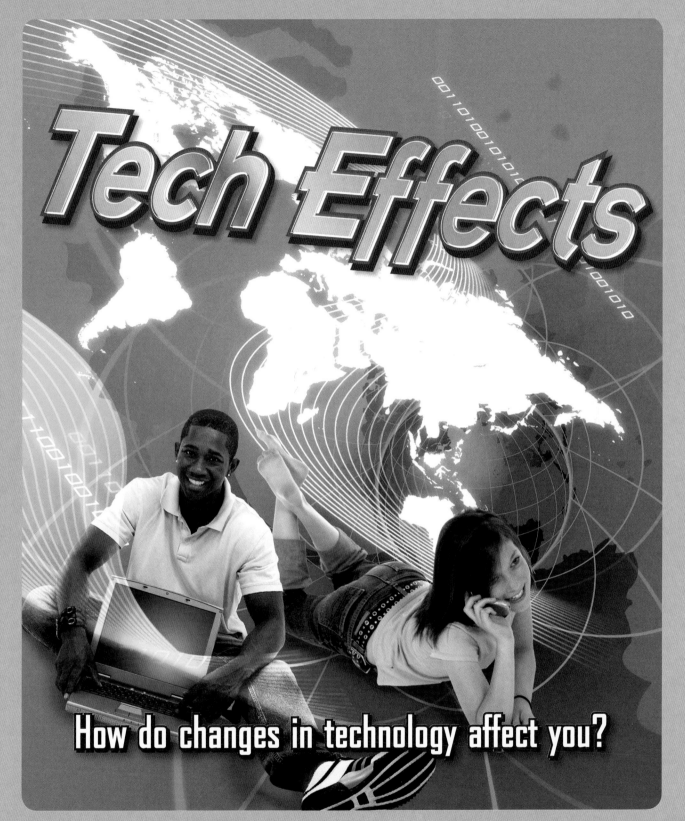

Tech Effects

How do changes in technology affect you?

Unit Learning Goals

- question text to increase understanding
- organize ideas in writing
- deliver oral presentations
- ask questions to evaluate media texts
- analyze narrative text pattern

Transfer Your Learning: Mathematics

How to ➤ Ask Questions

Good readers have a conversation with the text. They predict, make inferences, wonder about things, and ask lots of questions. There are three major types of questions:

Literal, **or "On the Line," Questions:** The answer is directly stated; it's given on the page.

Question: Who are the characters in the story "The Three Little Techies"?

Answer: So far, we know there are three computer technicians.

Inferential, **or "Between the Lines," Questions:** The answer is there in the text, but it's harder to find. You have to put together clues in the text with what you know to get an answer. Think about what the author implies as well as what is stated directly.

Question: When is this story set?

Answer: Despite the traditional "once upon a time" introduction, this story seems to be set in the present, since the main characters are computer technicians.

Evaluative, **or "Beyond the Lines," Questions:** These are often the toughest questions to answer because you're making a judgment or expressing a personal opinion using evidence from the text.

Question: How effective is the beginning of the story?

Answer: The beginning is good, because it sets a humorous tone and reminds the reader about the story of the three little pigs.

The Three Little Techies

Once upon a time, in a city far, far away, there lived three little computer technicians who thought they knew everything there was to know about computers. The first little techie decided she wanted to start her own company.

Transfer Your Learning

Across the Strands

Media Literacy: As you view or listen to a media text, use these three types of questions to analyze it. What type of question do you think will be the easiest to answer? Why?

Across the Curriculum

Mathematics: Asking questions plays a major role in solving problems. Keep track of the questions you ask yourself the next time you do math. Ask questions that are literal (such as "What am I being asked to solve in this problem?") and evaluative (such as "Does my answer make sense?").

Talk About It
What do you already know about virtual reality?

A Brief Introduction to Virtual Reality

Nonfiction Article by Sheila Wyborny

What is virtual reality (VR)? Some people describe virtual reality as a cartoon world that real people can visit. Virtual reality is the creation of 3-D environments with computers.

In VR you are immersed in an environment, you can navigate within it, and you can interact with objects in it. VR has helped people experience situations and events that might be difficult or impossible in the real world.

Asking Questions →

As you read, ask literal questions, the type of question where you can put your finger right on the answer. Ask yourself, "How does this author define virtual reality?"

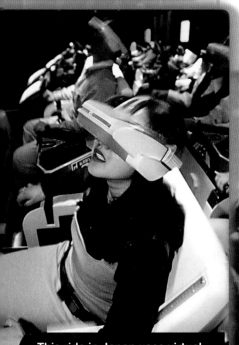

This ride in Japan uses virtual reality to increase the intensity of the experience.

Through virtual reality a person can walk among dinosaurs—without ever entering a time machine!

The technology of virtual reality has changed our world! VR makes it possible for people to go places and do things without ever leaving their homes. It lets people travel not only to different places, but to different times as well. Through virtual reality, a person can experience simulated events in history and meet famous people from earlier centuries.

A technician works on interior design using virtual reality.

Asking Questions →

As you read, ask inferential questions. Ask yourself, "What can I infer about the author's point of view from this paragraph?" Use the clues the author gave you and what you already know to make an inference.

Virtual reality has a great impact on many professions. Architects can see their designs before the buildings are constructed. They can "walk around" 3-D models of buildings and see them as if they physically existed in space. Their clients can also see the building designs more clearly.

Virtual Reality Glossary

robosurgeons: robots programmed to help in surgery or other medical operations

simulated: created to appear real

simulator: a machine or computer program that allows viewers to experience an event as if they were really there

telemedicine: using computer programs to perform surgery remotely—that is, the doctor can be in a hospital in Vancouver while the patient is in a hospital in Sudbury

3-D: three-dimensional, that is, seeming to have length, width, and depth (most images are only two-dimensional, having length and width but not depth)

virtual reality: a computer-created environment that is extremely realistic

Doctors can use VR to treat patients who live in remote areas and can't get to medical centres. Astronauts can use virtual reality programs to train for space missions. Law enforcement personnel can face life-threatening situations without actually being in harm's way. Pilots can practise difficult flight manoeuvres without any risk to aircraft or lives.

Virtual reality can also help students—for example, to prepare for future occupations. Students can use computer-aided design (CAD) programs to learn product design skills. Medical students can examine, diagnose, and even practise surgery on virtual patients. In Africa, VR simulations are being used to help people learn about activities as practical as beekeeping, water conservation, and malaria prevention.

Like other kinds of technology, virtual reality is constantly evolving and improving. Whereas the computers required for early virtual systems once took up the space of an entire room, some systems now fit in a space no bigger than a suitcase.

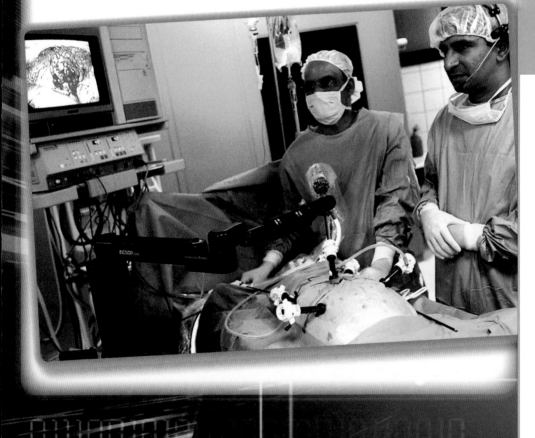

← **Asking Questions**

As you read, ask evaluative questions, the type of question that does not have an answer in the text. You need to form your own judgment or opinion. Ask yourself, "How would I feel about having a doctor operate on me using robot technology?"

Virtual Doctors Set Up Practice

One of the most amazing uses of virtual reality is in medicine. One technology, called *telemedicine*, allows a doctor to operate on a patient in a hospital thousands of kilometres away. Robots are used, either alone or to extend the skills of the human surgeon.

Soon robots will be able to do much more: One of the latest VR surgery simulators allows surgeons to practise complicated techniques before they actually enter an operating room. They can even feel when they've made a mistake. This technology is called "force feedback." It mimics how tissue and blood vessels feel and behave in real life. In the future, robosurgeons will be able to do this too.

As systems become more sophisticated, new uses for virtual reality are being discovered. For example, doctors can now use VR to diagnose heart defects in newborn babies. Flat images from body scanners are combined and turned into giant, rounded images of the child's heart. The VR heart images can highlight defects that might be missed by doctors studying conventional scans. Parents can also look at the 3-D images to better understand the defect.

The uses for virtual reality technology are only limited by our imaginations!

One of the most common uses of virtual reality is for entertainment in arcades.

When Science Fiction Becomes Reality

Virtual reality is a concept that keeps popping up in science fiction movies and TV shows. *The Matrix* is an example of a movie in which the virtual world is so realistic that the people living there think it is real.

In the TV series *Star Trek: The Next Generation*, the "Holodeck" is a sophisticated form of VR that allows people to take virtual vacations. Visiting the Holodeck allows crew members to go anywhere and anywhen in the galaxies. They can visit wonderful places, interact with virtual characters, and even eat virtual foods.

Asking Questions

A graphic organizer like this can help you to organize your questions.

Literal or "On the Line"	Inferencing or "Between the Lines"	Evaluative or "Beyond the Lines"

Reflecting

Questioning: What questions did you ask yourself as you read the article? Were you able to find answers to all your questions?

Metacognition: Think about the types of questions you asked yourself. What types of questions did you ask most often? What does this tell you about how you think about texts?

Critical Literacy: Does this article present a balanced and unbiased view of virtual reality? What evidence from the text supports your answer?

UNDER THE VIRTUAL WEATHER

Simulation by Christine Lau

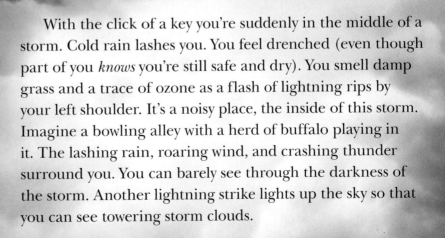

Imagine this. You're sitting in a warm, dry room in front of a computer. You put on a simple-looking headset that is remotely linked to the computer and the world you're about to enter.

With the click of a key you're suddenly in the middle of a storm. Cold rain lashes you. You feel drenched (even though part of you *knows* you're still safe and dry). You smell damp grass and a trace of ozone as a flash of lightning rips by your left shoulder. It's a noisy place, the inside of this storm. Imagine a bowling alley with a herd of buffalo playing in it. The lashing rain, roaring wind, and crashing thunder surround you. You can barely see through the darkness of the storm. Another lightning strike lights up the sky so that you can see towering storm clouds.

What was that? Out of the corner of your eye you catch sight of something disturbing. You flick your fingers to bring yourself closer and turn your head so that you can see better.

You see a twister forming within this storm system … swirling winds creating a spiral. Debris from the ground (dust, rocks, branches) is being picked up and carried away. With a twitch of your wrist you move the twister away from a populated town, toward a less-populated farmyard. Watch out, chickens!

You see a man and woman running for cover toward the storm cellar in the farmhouse. The woman clutches a portable radio. The man clutches a child. As the storm cellar doors swing shut the twister hits the farmhouse, lifts up the roof and carries it away, along with all of granny's precious things stored in the attic. Torrential rain washes out the recently planted crops.

As you follow the storm, you know that at least the family is safe. You glance back anyway, to make sure.

The Reality Behind Virtual Reality in Weather Forecasting

Virtual reality can help to forecast the weather. Satellites and weather balloons gather information about current weather systems. This information is used to create computer simulations. Computer programs can then predict how those systems will change and where they'll move. Scientists can study these simulations to learn more about various weather patterns. This information has helped to save lives and reduce the damage caused by severe weather systems.

Reflecting

Questioning: What questions did you ask as you read this selection? Were you able to find answers to your questions? If not, where can you look for answers?

Metacognition: At the beginning of this selection, you were asked to imagine something. What types of questions (literal, inferential, and/or evaluative) did you think of as a result of visualizing the storm? Why do you think that is?

Critical Thinking: How does the inset material on this page contribute to your understanding of the selection? Which type of text did you enjoy reading more: the simulation about being in the middle of a storm or the straightforward nonfiction about using virtual reality to understand weather? Why?

Talk About It

What do you think are some of the pros and cons of virtual schools?

Virtual school has everything but building

Newspaper Article by Mitchell Brown

It has a library, lesson plans, recess, report cards, and just about everything else you'd expect to find at an elementary school. Well, everything except the school itself.

Located in a strip mall in Newmarket, Ontario, LinkonLearning opened its virtual doors on December 9, 2002, to become Canada's first fully online elementary school.

Students who log on to the site can choose from about 10 000 lessons spread out over nine subject areas and every grade level from Junior Kindergarten to Grade 8.

An automated teacher's voice guides them through the lessons and praises them when they give the right answers. Students also have access to a virtual library in which they can "sign out" (download) reference books and short stories for assignments.

The program also rewards students who complete their lessons with time in the "playground," where they can play games and chat online with their friends.

Company president Janice Frohlich says they are targeting home-schooled children and children with conditions that make it difficult for them to learn in a traditional classroom setting, as well as students just looking for some extra tutoring.

Then there are the parents themselves, many of whom are looking for ways to cope with their children's ever-changing curriculum.

"We want to be able to give parents the tools to help their children," Ms. Frohlich says.

Ms. Frohlich and vice-president Mike Taylor teamed up in the mid-1990s to create an online educational program that could help their own children with their education.

It took them several years of studying curriculum plans from every province to develop what Ms. Frohlich calls "the red book."

Meanwhile, Mr. Taylor headed up a team of programmers working to build the site's backbone. That made it technically possible for students to submit their assignment answers, play a computerized trombone in the music room, or blend colours in a virtual art program.

Despite the breadth of the site's curriculum, Mr. Taylor says the site is not intended to be a complete substitute for teachers or parental guidance.

"We don't believe in replacing the school. That is not our intention," he says.

At least one parent is convinced of the site's ability to keep her children ahead of the curve. Truus Van Galen, a Newmarket mother of three, heard about the site in September 2001.

"Our kids are strong students anyway, but I find with this their general knowledge is getting broader," she says.

She feels that it's a good way to take advantage of children's desire to get on the computer as much as they can.

Another feature that pleases her is the ability for students to work at their own pace, adding that her Grade 3 daughter is already tackling several of the fourth-grade lesson plans with ease.

Ms. Frohlich says the company hopes to eventually introduce a French-language curriculum, high-school-level courses, and lesson plans incorporating sign language for hearing-impaired students.

For now, though, it's concentrating on getting the word out and showing elementary students and their parents what the site can do.

Reflecting

Questioning: What questions did you ask as you read this newspaper article? Did you find answers to all your questions? If not, where can you look for answers?

Metacognition: What questions did you ask that helped you understand this selection?

Critical Literacy: News reports should be objective. Is this article objective, or does it show a bias in favour of or against virtual schooling?

Talk About It
What makes text messaging more or less effective than other types of communications?

Is Txt Mightier

Newspaper Article from BBC News Online

When a 13-year-old Scottish girl handed in an essay written in text message shorthand, she explained to her flabbergasted teacher that it was easier than standard English.

She wrote: "My smmr hols wr CWOT. B4, we used 2go2 NY 2C my bro, his GF & thr 3 :-O kids FTF. ILNY, it's a gr8 plc." (In translation: "My summer holidays were a complete waste of time. Before, we used to go to New York to see my brother, his girlfriend, and their three screaming kids face to face. I love New York. It's a great place.")

The girl's teacher was not impressed, saying: "I could not believe what I was seeing. The page was riddled with hieroglyphics, many of which I simply could not translate."

Text messaging, e-mail, and computer spell-checks have long been blamed for declining standards of spelling and grammar.

Despite the advent of predictive text, which completes words as you write them, and even the launch of next-generation mobile networks, it seems that the simple texting skills people have learned in the last three or four years will be around for a while.

Already, text-message shortcuts have been adopted by those keen to get their point across in as little space as possible, be it advertising copy, poetry, or biblical passages.

It may be just a coincidence, but when invited to pick a classic text to read together for World Book Day, BBC[*] News Online readers voted for the slimmest volume on the list—*Heart of Darkness*, a dark but short read at a mere 96 pages.

[*]BBC is short for British Broadcasting Corporation

Than the Word?

In 1533, King Henry married Anne Boleyn :-)

One year later Henry became the head of the Church of England 0:-)

Just two years after that, he had Anne Boleyn executed for treason >:-0

I'M NOT SURE EMOTICONS BELONG IN A EUROPEAN HISTORY ESSAY, ZUMA.

YOU DON'T THINK THEY'RE CUTER THAN WORDS?

Zits comic strip by Jim Borgman and Jerry Scott

Rewritten in txt, Joseph Conrad's novel would be shorter still. Its opening line, "The *Nellie*, a cruising yawl, swung to her anchor without a flutter of the sails, and was at rest," might be condensed to "*T Neli*, a crzng yal, swng 2 hr anchr wout a fluta of T sails and was @ rest."

Could the Scottish schoolgirl be right? Could txt take over more of our expression because people simply find it easier than normal writing? Could this mean the liberation of our use of language?

Reflecting

Questioning: What questions did you ask about the newspaper article? What questions did you ask about the comic strip?

Metacognition: Which did you find it easier to develop questions for: the newspaper article or the comic strip? Why do you think that is?

Critical Thinking: Should the abbreviations used in text messaging become part of the official English language? How does the overuse of abbreviations and emoticons affect readers?

How to → Organize Ideas

When you're writing nonfiction, there are several organizational patterns to choose from. The following chart describes four of those patterns. The pattern you choose depends on your purpose.

Organizational Pattern	What It Means	Questions To Ask	Words Connected With This Pattern
Sequence EVENT → EVENT → EVENT	Events are told in order. Sometimes the order is chronological.	**What sequence of events is described?**	*first, second, third, then, next, after*
Cause and Effect CAUSE / EFFECT EFFECT OR EFFECT EFFECT \ CAUSE	Events are told in pairs, one event being caused by the other; for example, spilling pop on your computer may cause it to break down.	**What happened? What caused it to happen? Why or how did it happen?**	*because, as a result, in consequence, therefore*
Problem/Solution PROBLEM / SOLUTION SOLUTION	A problem is presented, and one or more solutions are suggested.	**What is the problem or problems? What are some possible solutions?**	*problem, dilemma, puzzling, solution, solve*
Compare and Contrast TOPICS ↓ SIMILARITIES ↓ DIFFERENCES	Two or more things are compared and/or contrasted. The text looks at differences and similarities.	**What is being compared? How are they alike? Different? What conclusion is drawn?**	*unlike, in comparison, by contrast, on the other hand, both … and …*

Transfer Your Learning

Across the Strands

Oral Communication: When you speak with others, you often choose an organizational pattern to make your ideas flow more logically. If you're explaining why you've decided to switch from an old computer to a new one, what pattern would you choose?

Across the Curriculum

History: History textbooks use more than one text pattern, depending on the topic. What pattern would you expect to find in the following sections?

• Long-Term Effects of the War of 1812

• Primary Causes of the War of 1812

• Events of the War of 1812

• An Interview with Laura Secord

Talk About It

What old-fashioned ideas or inventions do you think are going "the way of the dinosaur"?

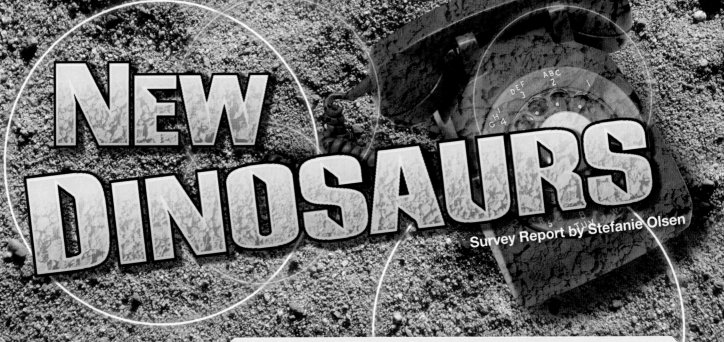

NEW DINOSAURS

Survey Report by Stefanie Olsen

Organizing Ideas →

Choose an organizational pattern that suits your purpose and topic. If you wanted to explain the effects technology has on everyday life, a cause-and-effect pattern would be most suitable. As you read, look for the characteristics of cause-and-effect text pattern.

The modern wired family is seeing a few mainstays going the way of the dinosaur: landlines, maps, newspapers, and, of course, the need to remember phone numbers or learn to spell.

That's according to a new study, called "The Digital Family," by cable network Nickelodeon. The findings are among the first to examine technology use in the home. They're part of a wider effort among researchers to understand how quickly changing technology is changing the family structure. They also want to observe the way kids communicate and are educated and entertained.

In 2006, Nickelodeon questioned parents of children from infants to 14-year-olds, as well as kids aged 6 to 14, about their use of TV, digital video recorders, video on demand, the Net, cellphones, video games, and MP3 players.

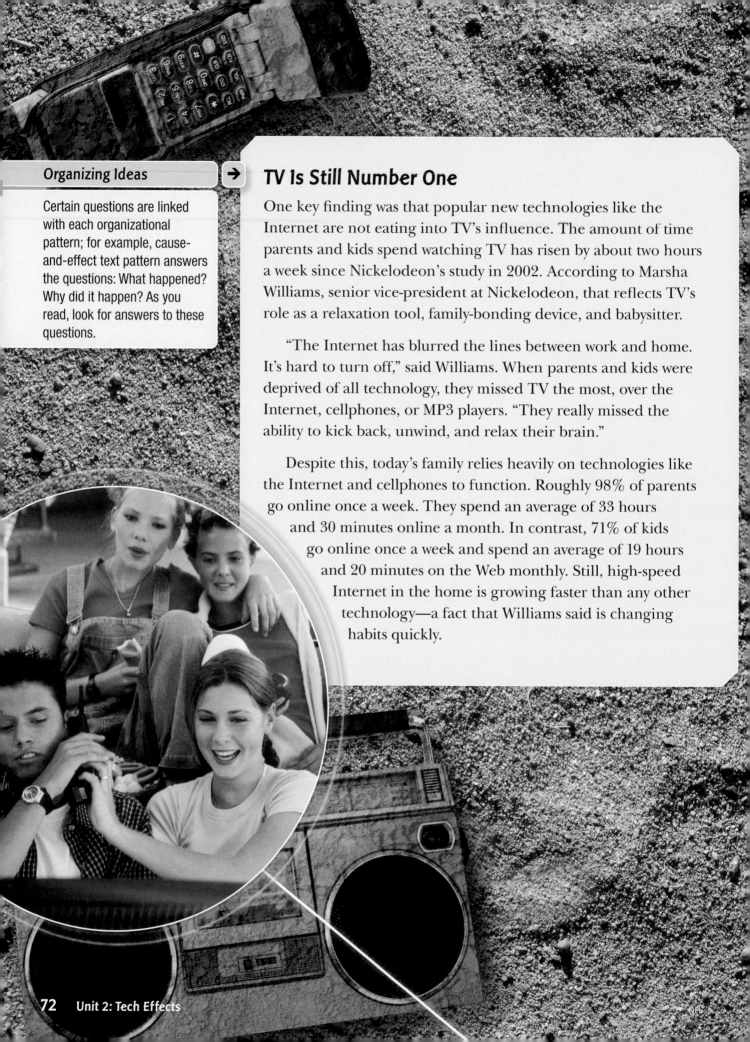

TV Is Still Number One

One key finding was that popular new technologies like the Internet are not eating into TV's influence. The amount of time parents and kids spend watching TV has risen by about two hours a week since Nickelodeon's study in 2002. According to Marsha Williams, senior vice-president at Nickelodeon, that reflects TV's role as a relaxation tool, family-bonding device, and babysitter.

"The Internet has blurred the lines between work and home. It's hard to turn off," said Williams. When parents and kids were deprived of all technology, they missed TV the most, over the Internet, cellphones, or MP3 players. "They really missed the ability to kick back, unwind, and relax their brain."

Despite this, today's family relies heavily on technologies like the Internet and cellphones to function. Roughly 98% of parents go online once a week. They spend an average of 33 hours and 30 minutes online a month. In contrast, 71% of kids go online once a week and spend an average of 19 hours and 20 minutes on the Web monthly. Still, high-speed Internet in the home is growing faster than any other technology—a fact that Williams said is changing habits quickly.

For example, deprived of the Internet for 10 days, many parents and kids found that being online is more essential than they had thought for accessing information, doing schoolwork, or staying in touch with friends.

"Moms who gave up the Internet were very annoyed," Williams said. One mom was exasperated by, as a consequence of giving up the Internet, having to visit an office to put money on a highway toll card. "It was so inconvenient for her." One student had to take a trip to the library to finish a report on China.

As a result, Internet technology is changing behaviours at home. The study showed that, thanks to the Internet, a quarter of parents believe it's no longer necessary to spell well, use printed dictionaries, or read the newspaper. Fewer kids ages 8 to 14 agreed (an average of one-fifth), except when it came to printed maps. About 20% of parents, versus 21% of kids, said they no longer need to know how to read a geographic map.

While TV and the Net are very popular, many other habits and technologies are losing out in the modern family.

The Cellphone Effect

Because of cellphones, almost half of all kids and parents say they therefore don't need to remember phone numbers anymore. More than a third say the landline isn't needed. And a quarter of kids (and 16% of parents) say the spontaneity of mobile phones means it's not important to plan ahead (89% of parents own a cellphone versus 61% of kids ages 12 to 14.)

Parents and Cellphones

— 11% of parents don't have cellphones

89% of parents have cellphones

Children and Cellphones

39% of kids don't have cellphones

61% of kids have cellphones

Because of MP3 players, a third of kids say it's no longer necessary to make casual conversation with others or listen to the radio. More than half of parents, and 45% of kids, say they don't need to buy CDs or albums.

The research also shows that technology in the home is a two-way street—kids use new technology and, as a result, their parents adopt it and vice versa. Parents are just as likely as their kids, if not more so, to embrace cellphones, MP3 players, and the Net.

In a surprising finding, more parents (68%) use game consoles, compared with 58% of 8- to 14-year-olds. That's likely because parents are using game consoles to bond with their kids, according to Williams.

For parents, the cellphone is all-important for keeping tabs on kids. It was commonly described as an "electronic leash." Nearly half of parents surveyed said they wanted to get their child a cellphone because it helped them reach the child at all times. The common rule among parents is: "no matter when or where I call, you answer the phone or you lose it," according to Williams.

Other observations in the study included

- Williams called the family unit today the smartest generation of consumers ever, because parents and kids seek information about products on the Net.

- In Nickelodeon's study of parents and kids who did not have access to any "screen" for 10 days, what parents said they missed most was TV and its pure escapism.

- Just because it's possible to converge cellphones and MP3 players doesn't mean it's practical for digital families. Doing so isn't compatible with the different ways parents and kids use the individual devices. Parents use cellphones for checking in with their kids and MP3 players for tuning out. Kids use cellphones to talk to their friends.

←

Organizing Ideas

Certain key words are connected with each text pattern. What key words help you identify the text pattern this author chose?

Reflecting

Reading Like a Writer: Do you think this author chose the correct text pattern for her topic and purpose? What other text pattern would have worked? Why do you think so?

Metacognition: How has technology changed how you learn or think? What preparation would you need to complete if you were to write an effective cause-and-effect article answering this question?

Critical Literacy: Are the findings in this survey report supported by your own experience? Who do you think is not represented in this survey? Think about the effect on the reader of how numbers are reported. For example, why does the author say "21% of kids say they no longer need to read a geographic map" rather than saying "79% of kids say they still need to read a geographic map"?

NO-TECH

Advice Column by Brad Tanzini

Dear Brad,

We don't have the Internet at home. We live in the country and my mom says it's too expensive and it would be too slow anyway. But other kids at my school all seem so connected to each other and the Internet. Sometimes it feels like I don't fit in.

Now that I'm in Grade 7, this problem seems even bigger than it did last year. I have lots of homework that the other kids in my class seem able to handle. They say they're finding a lot of the information they need on the Net. Without the Internet, how am I going to study for reports and tests?

I have a couple of friends down the road who feel the same way. What can we do when we're in the no-tech zone?

Tech Lost,
Courtney Warren

Dear Tech Lost,

Courtney, I hope I can help you. I know it's hard for kids when they feel like outsiders at school. Feeling connected to your peers is important.

There's still a lot that you can do to feel connected—even if you can't share Internet experiences. For example:

• When your classmates talk about stuff they do on the Internet, you can still listen. People love to talk.

• Tell them about the stuff you do at home. They may never have had the chance to do the things you do either.

• Talk about music, sports, or TV shows.

• Invite some of your classmates over to your house to enjoy an evening in the "no-tech zone." Play cards or board games, go out and watch the stars, or have a skating party.

ZONE

- Make friends (like you've already done) with other kids in the same boat. You might be surprised at how many other kids in your school don't spend any time, or much time, on the Internet.

Your other problem is how to keep up with the schoolwork. Some of the solutions to this problem might also help you to feel more connected. For example:

- Your local or school library will have lots of books and may even have computers you can use.

- Get a few study partners that live in town. If you can, spend a few hours every week at their places using their computers to do homework together.

- If you have the time and permission, start doing odd jobs in your neighbourhood to make some money. Maybe one day soon you'll be able to help your mom pay for Internet access.

Well, I hope you find one of these tips helpful.

Thanks for writing,
Brad

Reflecting

Reading Like a Writer: Advice columns usually use a problem/solution text pattern. What features of problem/solution text pattern do you notice in this selection?

Critical Thinking: What do you think is the hardest part of writing an advice column?

Questioning: What types of questions did you ask as you read this selection: on the line, between the lines, or beyond the lines? How did asking questions help you understand the selection?

Talk About It
What do you picture when you think of the word *robot*?

The New Workplace

Nonfiction Text from *Cool Stuff and How It Works*

In the last few decades, computers have changed the way society is organized. Any job that can be broken down into a series of simple steps can be taken over by a computer or a robot designed for a specific task, such as spray-painting a car. Robots can do most of the repetitive and risky tasks in factories. As a result, factory workers spend less time on the production line.

In offices, computers process much of the repetitive work, such as calculating figures and printing out documents. Laser printers and scanners save time and increase productivity. Thanks to the laptop and the cellphone, office workers are less tied to their desks than they used to be.

Some jobs can only be done by humans. The decisions that doctors have to make, for example, are too complex and subtle for a computer—doctors need to diagnose and treat patients in person.

Robot Worker

Industrial robots have been used in factory assembly lines since 1961. Almost one million robots work in industry today. Robots mainly work on car assembly lines, but they also work in many warehouses, hospitals, and laboratories. They perform many tasks that people find boring or dangerous, such as those inside nuclear reactors or clearing land mines.

Nanorobots are a new generation of microscopic robots. These tiny robots could one day travel through human arteries, looking for defects or obstructions.

Robart III is a robotic security guard developed by the U.S. Navy. It can find intruders, chase them, photograph them, and fire a non-lethal dart. The main challenge facing this type of robot is how to determine the level of threat a trespasser really poses, and respond appropriately.

How the Robart III Works

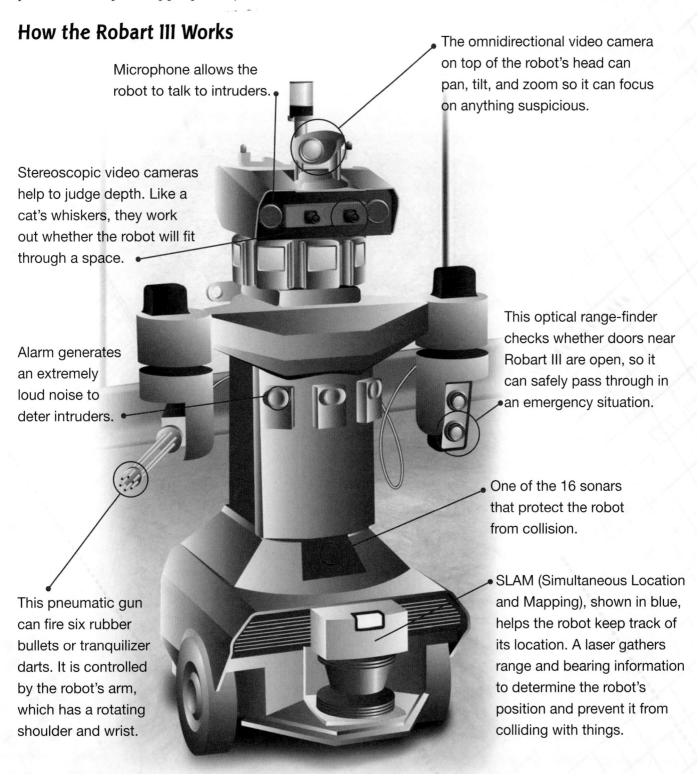

Microphone allows the robot to talk to intruders.

The omnidirectional video camera on top of the robot's head can pan, tilt, and zoom so it can focus on anything suspicious.

Stereoscopic video cameras help to judge depth. Like a cat's whiskers, they work out whether the robot will fit through a space.

Alarm generates an extremely loud noise to deter intruders.

This optical range-finder checks whether doors near Robart III are open, so it can safely pass through in an emergency situation.

One of the 16 sonars that protect the robot from collision.

This pneumatic gun can fire six rubber bullets or tranquilizer darts. It is controlled by the robot's arm, which has a rotating shoulder and wrist.

SLAM (Simultaneous Location and Mapping), shown in blue, helps the robot keep track of its location. A laser gathers range and bearing information to determine the robot's position and prevent it from colliding with things.

Robot Surgery

Surgical robots were invented in the 1980s. They combined robotic arms with surgical viewing devices called *endoscopes*.

Robotic arms enter the body through tiny incisions and perform delicate surgical procedures with complete precision. The robot is operated by a surgeon, using a remote-control system.

The high-speed transmission of computer images and data makes it possible for doctors to carry out robot surgery on patients in hospitals thousands of kilometres away.

How Robot Surgery Works

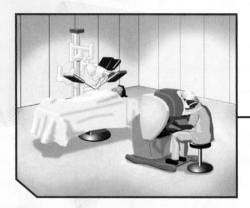

A surgical robot has two main parts: a robotic arm unit, which is positioned over the patient, and a control console several feet away. During an operation, the surgeon sits at the console, watching the procedure through a magnified viewfinder and guiding the robot arms with his/her hands. Assistants and an anesthetist (a doctor who puts patients to sleep before an operation) may also be present.

A camera attached to one of the robot's arms takes images inside the incision and relays them to the magnified viewfinder, which creates sharp, 3-D images. The view is much clearer than is possible with the naked eye. Sophisticated joysticks translate the surgeon's hand movements into far smaller, precise movements of the robotic arms. The system can eliminate any tremors in the surgeon's hands and improve accuracy.

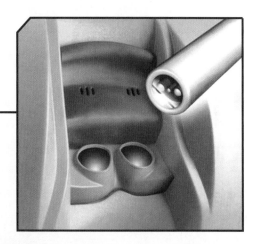

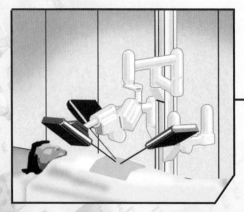

The stainless steel robot arms enter the skin through three small incisions, each no wider than the thickness of a pencil. While the camera at the tip of one arm films the operation, other surgical instruments are used to cut, hold, and stitch. When not in use, the arms are rock steady. This reduces the level of trauma for the patient.

Capsule Camera

The capsule camera is a miniature video camera you can swallow like a pill. It has provided the first real look inside a functioning small intestine and is able to diagnose gastrointestinal disorders. Researchers call it a "gutbot." As it passes through the body, the capsule films the inside of the small intestine.

How the Capsule Camera Works

One of the trickiest parts of the body to examine is the small intestine. It is 6 m long, but doctors can see only the first third using an endoscope (a flexible tube with a light at one end). However, with a capsule camera, the entire length of the small intestine can be filmed in colour. The capsule is a miracle of miniaturization. It incorporates a digital camera, light source, and radio transmitter in a streamlined package not much bigger than a pill. It passes slowly through the small intestine, taking two pictures every second. The images are transmitted as radio waves to a receiver worn on a belt. The receiver also records the camera's location, so doctors can pinpoint any abnormality.

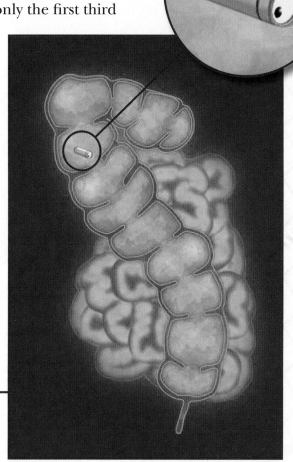

This X-ray reveals the twists and turns of the human intestines. Natural contractions of the small intestine's walls push the capsule (2.5 cm long and 1.25 cm wide) through the body. The capsule camera takes around 50 000 images.

Reflecting

Reading Like a Writer: What text pattern did the author choose for this selection? How effective do you think that choice was?

Metacognition: How do the headings and visuals help you to understand the material in this selection?

Critical Literacy: As you read this article, what opinion did you form about the authors' credibility? Did you decide the authors knew what they were talking about? What in the text helped you form your opinion?

 How to **Deliver Presentations**

Oral presentations can seem challenging. Here are a few ways to make them easier.

1. Carefully plan your presentation, considering your purpose and audience. For example, how will a presentation to your class reviewing your favourite sci-fi novel be different from a presentation to your school on the importance of new school computers?

2. As you plan, think about how your topic affects your structure and style. For example, a presentation describing your favourite video game is going to be different from a presentation on the effects of violence in video games.

Topic	Favourite Video Game	Effects of Violent Video Games
Purpose	to entertain	to persuade
Audience	class	school
Text Pattern	descriptive	cause/effect
Style	informal	formal

3. As you speak, remember to use vocal effects, such as

   • speaking slowly, clearly, and loudly enough that everyone hears you

   • speaking with expression and enthusiasm

   • pausing before or after important points

4. Use visual aids (such as images, charts, props, or video clips) to support your presentation.

Transfer Your Learning

Across the Strands

Writing: How is delivering an oral presentation similar to writing a report? What important steps should you remember in both situations?

Across the Curriculum

Health: How would you speak about an important health topic, such as tooth decay, to an audience of students your age? How would you change your approach if you were speaking to a Grade 1 class?

Talk About It
When was the last time an adult told you to play a lot of computer games?

Gamer Jobs

Oral Presentation by Lesley Milner

Delivering Presentations →

A good oral presentation is carefully planned, keeping purpose and audience in mind. What is Lesley's purpose and who is her audience?

Delivering Presentations →

In an oral presentation, topic can affect structure and style. Think about the structure and style Lesley uses.

The following text comes from a presentation Lesley Milner gave to students about her job in the computer industry. Lesley is a Project Manager at Digital Extremes in London, Ontario.

Thank you for asking me to speak with you about my job. I *love* to talk about what I do for a living because *I love my job!* I work in the exciting world of video games. I get to oversee a video game from its earliest stages of development to the final product on sale at your local video-game store.

I'm the project manager at Digital Extremes. I keep the team working together, so that all the staff—from the art department to the programmers to the designers—know their responsibilities and are working toward the same goal. I make sure the project gets finished ... on time and on budget.

I've worked in the gaming industry for ten years. To tell you the truth, I never dreamed of having this type of job. I went to school for journalism and worked in the magazine industry after I graduated.

It's a complete fluke that I ended up working with video games. About ten years ago, I got laid off from this small magazine I was working at. A friend of mine got me a job at a company that was making video games. They wanted someone to write, edit, and design a book for a game they were developing. That became my first job in the industry. At first it was just a temporary position but it turned into a full-time job. Soon, I was editing and writing text for game manuals, in-game text, missions, and overviews. It was *great* because I could use my writing skills.

I really love what I do, and I love working in this industry. The upside of this industry is that it has a really creative atmosphere and we all work together as a team. I have a chance to share my best ideas with others. And they share their ideas with me.

Unfortunately, one downside of this industry is that it's *volatile*—companies go bust and change owners often. If you want to work in this industry, be prepared to change companies *often*!

Some of you will be pleased to know that playing video games helped me get and keep this job! When I was younger I played the arcade-type games, like Pacman and Donkey Kong, but I never really thought much about how they worked or who made those kinds of things. Once I got into the industry I started playing games like Starcraft, Doom, Quake, and Half-Life. I know *a lot* about games, both as a player and as someone who works in the industry. It's important for everyone who works on a game to keep the players in mind. If players don't like our games, we won't make any money!

I'm not as much of a "gamer" as most of the people who work here. The designers are the *real* gamers; those of us who work in production don't get a lot of time to play! Still, we all have our favourite games. One of my favourites, and a game I'm very proud to have been part of developing, is Company of Heroes.

Delivering Presentations

Good speakers use vocal effects to deliver a smooth presentation. For example, they speak slowly, clearly, and loudly, or pause before important ideas. Where do you think Lesley would have paused in this presentation?

My advice to any of you who want to work in the gaming industry is to play a lot of games! Seriously—you need to know what makes a game fun. You should also have good analytical skills. You need to introduce yourself to the gaming community early on by getting involved in a *Mod*. (*Mod* is short for *modeller* or *modification*. Gamers who know how can modify the game in some way—adding elements like different characters—and tell other gamers how to do so.) Learn to evaluate a good game and a bad game. There are also some good college courses that can help to get you started in the industry. Good luck!

← **Delivering Presentations**

Speakers often use visual aids to support their presentation. What visual aids do you think Lesley could have used in her presentation?

Reflecting

Delivering Presentations: What evidence is there in the selection that Lesley is considering her purpose and audience as she speaks?

Questioning: What questions did you ask yourself as you read this selection? If you were present when Lesley spoke, what questions would you have wanted to ask?

Connecting to Other Media: Think about what you know about producing movies or TV shows. What information in this selection connects with what you know about producing those types of media?

Talk About It
What are the signs you've been playing computer games too long?

CONFESSIONS OF A GAMER

Monologue by Haley Fam

Let me tell you when I realized I had a problem. I couldn't stand up. I'd been sitting at my computer for almost four hours straight, playing this new game, Zorgah's Revenge. Finally, I had to go to the bathroom, so I paused the play and I stood up. I should say that *I tried to stand up.* You know how your legs can feel all numb if you've been sitting curled up for too long. I had to pound my legs with my fists to get the feeling back.

Of course my hands were all cramped from holding the controller and thumbing buttons. It took me a lot of fumbling to undo the button and zipper on my pants ... ok, that's definitely TMI! LOL!

As well, once I moved my eyes away from the screen, all I could see were little spaceships, zapping across the galaxy.

Speaking of eyes, at night I closed my eyes and all I could see were images from the computer game: characters in bright costumes battling it out on a black screen. I woke up every morning with my hands curled up as if I were still gripping the controller! Clear signs. I. HAD. A. PROBLEM.

I wasn't taking this problem seriously ... until I started calling my friends and family by the names of characters! It's not too bad when you call your best friend of 14 years by the name of a game hero: Vitrella Victorious.

My mom really didn't appreciate being called by the villain's name: Zorgah! My dad got extremely zorked off when I told him that his tofu casserole deserved to be annihilated by a Zork cannon.

So I decided to take a break. Summer had arrived, maybe it was time to spend a few hours outside. Plus, Mom and Dad were in total agreement about the punishment for not studying for my final exams and playing computer games instead. I was banned from the computer for the entire summer.

I knew I could totally go cold turkey on computer games. I was in control. Time to sit outside with my friend and just relax.

The first day was great, just my thumbs twitching a bit, my eyes going astray, looking for enemy aircraft. Sure, I could so master this!

I don't know how I ended up clutching my friend's new cellphone, playing games. I didn't even notice when it started raining or when she went home. Ok, confession time ... me + computer games = problem.

Reflecting

Communicating Effectively: From the speaker's language, what can you tell about her audience? Do you think she's speaking to friends, family, a small group, or a large group? What makes you think so? What is the speaker's purpose?

Metacognition: Haley makes her purpose clear and uses language that gains the audience's attention. When you speak to an audience, what do you do to gain and focus attention? When you listen to a speaker, what vocal effects help you focus?

Connecting to Other Media: With what other media could you imagine having this kind of problem? What symptoms of the problem would you have?

How to > Evaluate Media Texts

When you evaluate a media text, you have to think carefully about the text and form an opinion or judgment about it. You need to look for clues in the text that tell you about the point of view and what the producers believe or value.

Media texts come in many forms: ads, blogs, podcasts, CD covers, songs, websites, newspapers, TV shows, movies. Whatever form it is you're evaluating, many of the same important questions can be asked.

First, think about the purpose, audience, and message of the media text.

Use questions like these:

• Who produced the media text?

• What is the purpose and audience of the media text?

• What effect did the producers want the media text to have?

• What are the **explicit messages** in the media text?

• What are the **implicit messages** in the media text?

• What do the producers of the text believe or value? How does that compare with what you believe or value?

Explicit messages are those surface messages that you spot immediately. For example, "This toothpaste makes your teeth whiter."

Implicit messages are not as obvious. You may have to "read between the lines" to understand implicit messages. For example, "Having white teeth makes you more popular" may be the implicit message in a toothpaste ad.

Next, think about the methods used to achieve this purpose. Use questions like these:

- What first catches your eye about this media text?

- What choices were made in creating this media text? For example, colours, music, fonts, camera angles, special effects, sound effects, or cropping of images.

- What is the intended effect of these media techniques? For example, if a producer places the camera at floor level and shoots upward, people look bigger, as they do in this image from a sci-fi movie.

- How does the media text urge the audience to feel or act?

Finally, put all this information together and form an opinion or judgment about the media text.

Transfer Your Learning

Across the Strands

Reading: What questions from above can you also ask when you're reading a text with maps or photos? Why is it important to consider the author's purpose?

Across the Curriculum

History: Which of the above questions are also important to ask as you view media texts in History class?

Talk About It

What makes you try out a computer game—the cover, the advertising, a recommendation, a review you've read?

JUDGING BY THE COVER

Evaluating Media Texts →

Video Game Packages from various sources

When you evaluate a media text, you have to think carefully about the text and form an opinion or make a judgment about it. You need to look for clues in the text that tell you about its point of view and what the producers believe or value. As you examine these covers, ask yourself questions like those on pages 88 and 89.

Evaluating Media Texts →

Identify the purpose and audience for the media text. The purpose of a video game cover is to sell the game. How effective do you think this game cover is? What audience do you think this cover would appeal to?

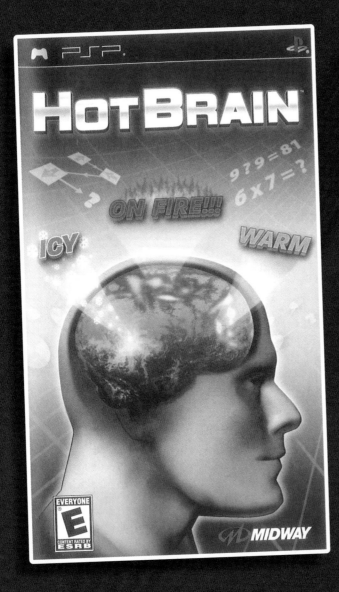

← **Evaluating Media Texts**

Identify the explicit and implicit messages in the media text. For example, the explicit message on this cover is that this is a game about problem solving. The implicit message is that it is for clever people. How do you respond to these explicit and implicit messages?

↖ **Evaluating Media Texts**

Think about the methods or techniques the media text uses to achieve its purpose. For example, both cool (blue) and warm (red) colours are used on this cover, as well as the words *hot*, *warm*, and *fire*. What effect does this have on you?

Reflecting

Media Literacy: Which of these covers do you think is most effective? Why do you think so? Give your opinion or judgment for one of these media texts.

Metacognition: What questions did you ask yourself as you viewed these covers? What strategies helped you identify the implicit messages communicated on these covers?

Connecting to Other Media: How do you think the production of video game covers is similar to or different from the production of book covers?

Talk About It
How would you feel about a computer game if someone told you that playing it would be good for you?

SERIOUS PLAYING

Online Article by Linda J. Phipps

Are you tired of video games in which all you do is shoot at spaceships or pretend you're a wizard? Have you ever wanted to work on the International Space Station? What about working in a refugee camp? Saving people from deadly diseases? Working as a peacekeeper in a war zone? Helping people after disaster strikes?

If you answered *yes* to any of these questions, then there are some video games that you need to check out. *Serious* video games. These games take on the real world and deal with complex issues.

Serious games can be entertaining but their main mission is to teach or train players. Suzanne Seggerman, co-founder of Games for Change, says, "Video games are being used for more serious purposes. These games illustrate complex situations."

It turns out, serious games can have surprising as well as positive effects. For example, Re-Mission is a game designed for cancer patients. Players control a microscopic character with a med blaster who goes through the game blasting away disease and infection. In studies, cancer patients who played this game showed higher levels of antibodies and chemotherapy drugs in their blood than patients who played other fun games.

Food Force is a role playing game that allows players to become virtual-aid workers, handing out food in areas struck by disaster. Produced by the United Nations' World Food Programme in April 2005, the game is free to download. Since its creation, Food Force has been downloaded more than five million times.

Food Force's project manager, Silke Buhr, says everyone was surprised by how successful the game was. "No humanitarian aid organization has built a game like this before, so we really couldn't have known."

Players of Food Force "learn that kids all over the world are the same and that kids their own age go hungry," says Bob March, a serious-game advocate, "If we teach kids a little bit of social responsibility, they'll incorporate it into the rest of their lives.... Some of them will go on to create games, and it'll create a snowball effect."

There are many other serious games. Peacemaker is a game in which players try to resolve the Israeli-Palestinian crisis in the Middle East. Asi Burak developed Peacemaker with a team of others. He reports, "Players get very engaged. They really try very hard to get a solution. Even after two hours, they'd say they know more about the conflict now than after reading newspapers for ten years."

Video games can be more persuasive than other texts. They allow players to experience the world from a different perspective. Henry Jenkins, a professor who studies games and learning, points out, "The generation that grew up with Super Mario is entering the workplace and entering politics, so they see games as just another tool to use to communicate."

Playing Just For Fun
Interview by Corry Codner

For this interview Corry questioned long-time gamer Maureen Olivia de Sousa.

Corry: How long have you been playing games?
Maureen: Since I was 11, over 20 years. I started with an Atari 2600 and since then I've had seven game consoles, not including handhelds.

Corry: Why do you like to play video games?
Maureen: Video games help me escape daily life. After a hard day, I vent my frustration by playing boxing or racing games or an RPG (role playing game).

Corry: What about serious video games? Don't you think they're just as much fun?
Maureen: They remind me too much of reality. I play to escape.

Corry: But have you ever played a serious game?
Maureen: Sure, a few times. I've played Trauma Centre, where you have to stitch up wounds and operate on people. You're saving lives. But I don't find it a lot of fun. I'm competitive. I like playing games with fast action, not thinking. If I want to think, I read a book.

Reflecting

Media Literacy: Look for clues that tell you what the people in each text (both the online article and the interview) value and believe. Think about your beliefs and values. Give your opinion or judgment about this topic and the media texts.

Metacognition: What information in this online article did you have trouble understanding?

What questions did you ask yourself as you read? How would playing these games focus your ideas for writing an opinion piece about serious video games?

Connecting to Other Media: How are these games like or unlike the video games you enjoy? Would you play these games? Why or why not?

Narrative

A straightforward narrative follows this pattern:

1. **Introduction:** the writer introduces characters, setting, and problem or conflict.

2. **Rising Action:** a series of events develop the problem or conflict.

3. **Climax:** tension builds to the point where the character(s) succeed or fail at solving the problem.

4. **Falling Action:** the action falls rapidly after the highest point of tension.

5. **Resolution** or **Denouement:** falling action leads to the ending. Stories may sometimes include a surprise ending.

Complex narratives may have multiple plot lines, that is, there is more than one story being told that may or may not connect to the other stories.

climax

rising action

falling action

introduction

resolution

Narrative has five elements:

- **characters:** who we learn about through the author's descriptions, what the characters think, say, or do, and what others think or say about them

- **setting:** the time and place in which the action happens

- **plot:** the action or events in the story; where a problem or conflict is resolved

- **theme:** the story's big idea(s)—for example, survival or growing up

- **perspective:** the point of view of the narrator (person telling the story)

Transfer Your Learning

Across the Strands

Media Literacy: Movies often use the same narrative structure you find in stories and novels. What movie have you seen recently that uses a straightforward narrative text pattern? What movie have you seen that uses a more complex narrative text pattern with several plot lines? Which movie did you prefer? Why?

Across the Curriculum

History: Sometimes you'll have the opportunity to read a fictional story based on historical events. How could a novel about settlers in New France help you understand what you learn in history class? Why would it also be important to read nonfiction texts about the subject?

Talk About It
If something seems too good to be true, it probably is!

Lose Now, Pay Later

Short Story by Carol Farley

I think my little brother is crazy. At least I hope he is. Because if his loony idea is right, then all of us are being used like a flock of sheep, and that's a pretty gruesome thought. Humans just can't be that stupid. My brother has a dumb idea, that's all. It's just a dumb idea.

This whole situation started about eight months ago. That's when I first knew anything about it, I mean. My best friend, Trinja, and I were shopping when we noticed a new store where an old insurance office used to be. It was a cubbyhole, really, at the far end of the mall where hardly anybody ever goes. We were there because we'd used that entrance as we came home from school.

"Swoodies!" Trinja said, pointing at the letters written across the display window. "What do you think they are, Deb?"

I stared through the glass. The place had always looked dim and dingy before, full of desks, half-dead plants, and bored-looking people; but now it was as bright and glaring as a Health Brigade Corp office. There weren't any people inside at all, but there were five or six gold-coloured machines lining the walls. Signs were hung everywhere.

SWEETS PLUS GOODIES = SWOODIES, one said. Flavours were posted by each machine: peanut-butter-fudge-crunch, butter-rum-pecan, chocolate-nut-mint. Things like that. The biggest sign of all simply said *free.*

I have to admit that the place gave me the creeps that first time I saw it. I don't know why. It just looked so bare and bright, so empty and clean, without any people or movement. The glare almost hurt my eyes. And I guess I was suspicious about anything that was completely free. Still, though, there was a terrific aroma drifting out of there—sort of a combination of all those flavours that were listed on the signs.

"Let's go in," Trinja said, grabbing my arm. I could see that the smell was getting to her, too. She's always on a diet, so she thinks about food a lot.

"But it's so empty in there," I said, drawing away.

"They've just opened, that's all," she told me, yanking my arm again. "Besides, machines and robots run lots of the stores. Let's go inside and see what's in there."

Do you know that wonderful spurt of air that rushes out when you first open an expensive box of candy? The inside of that store smelled just like the inside of one of those boxes. For a few seconds we just stood there sniffing and grinning. My salivary glands started swimming.

Trinja turned toward the nearest machine. "Coconut-almond-marshmallow." She was almost drooling. "I've got to try one, Deb." She pressed the button, and a chocolate cone dropped down, like a coffee cup from a kitcho machine. Then a mixture, similar to the look of soft ice cream, filled it. "Want to try it with me?" she asked, reaching for the cone. We both took a taste.

Narrative Text Pattern →

Rising Action: A series of events develop the problem or conflict. What important event happens in the first part of the story? What seems to be the problem? As you read, think about how each event contributes to the story's building tension.

It was absolutely the neatest sensation I've had in my whole life. Swoodies aren't cold like ice cream or warm like cooked pudding, but they're a blend of both in temperature and texture. The flavour melts instantly, and your whole mouth and brain are flooded with tastes and impressions. Like that first swoodie I tried, coconut-almond-marshmallow; suddenly, as my mouth separated the individual tastes, my brain burst into memories associated with each flavour.

I felt as if I were lying on a warm beach, all covered with coconut suntan oil—then I heard myself giggling and singing as a group of us roasted marshmallows around a campfire—then I relived the long-ago moments of biting into the special Christmas cookies my grandmother made with almonds when I was little.

"Wow!" Trinja looked at me, and I could see that she had just experienced the same kind of reactions. We scarfed up the rest of that swoodie in just a few more bites, and we moved on to another flavour. With each one it was the same. I felt a combination of marvellous tastes and joyous thoughts. We tried every flavour before we finally staggered out into the mall again.

"I'll have to diet for a whole year now," Trinja said, patting her stomach.

"I feel like a blimp myself," I told her, but neither one of us cared. We both felt terrific. "Go ahead in there," I called to some kids who were looking at the store. "You'll love those swoodies."

"It's a publicity stunt, we think," Trinja told them. "Everything is free in there."

In no time at all the news about the swoodie shop had spread all over town. But days passed, and still everything was absolutely free. Nobody knew who the new owners were or why they were giving away their product. Nobody cared. The mall directors said a cheque arrived to pay for the rent, and that was all they were concerned about. The Health Brigade Corp said swoodies were absolutely safe for human consumption.

SWOODIE

← **Narrative Text Pattern**

Rising Action: A series of events develop the problem or conflict. Sometimes, writers hint at the problem without stating it explicitly. Is the problem more obvious now? What do you think will happen next?

Swoodies were still being offered free a month later, but the shop owners had still not appeared. By then nobody cared. There were always long lines of people in front of the place, but the swoodies tasted so good nobody minded waiting for them. And the supply was endless. Soon more shops like the first one began opening in other places around the city, with machines running in the same quiet, efficient way. And everything was still absolutely free.

Soon all of us were gaining weight like crazy.

"It's those swoodies," Trinja told me as we left the mall after our daily binge. "I can't leave them alone. Each one must have a thousand calories, but I still pig out on them."

I sighed as I walked out into the sunshine. "Me too. If only there was some easy way to eat all the swoodies we want and still not gain any weight!"

The words were hardly out of my mouth when I noticed a new feature in the mall parking lot. Among all the usual heliobiles there was a tall white plastic box, sort of like those big telephone booths you see in old pictures. A flashing sign near the booth said *The Slimmer*. A short, thin woman was standing beside it. She was deeply tanned and her head was covered with a green turban almost the same colour as the jumpsuit she was wearing.

Trinja looked at the sign, then glanced at the woman. "What's that mean?"

"It means that this machine can make you slimmer," the woman answered. She had a deep, strange-sounding voice. "Just step inside and you'll lose unwanted fat."

She seemed so serious and confident that I was startled. In the old days people thought they could lose weight in a hurry, but those of us who live in 2041 aren't that gullible. No pills or packs or wraps or special twenty-four hour diets can work. There isn't any easy way to get rid of fat, and that's all there is to it. I knew this booth was a scam or a joke of some kind, but the woman acted as if it was a perfectly respectable thing. Her seriousness sort of unnerved me. I looked into the booth half expecting someone to jump out laughing. But it was empty, stark white, and, except for some overhead grillwork, it was completely smooth and bare.

Narrative Text Pattern ➜

Introduction: Setting and characters are introduced at the beginning, but sometimes writers don't immediately reveal everything. What inferences have you already made about the setting? What new information about setting do you learn in this section?

"How can a thing like this make you slimmer?" I asked.

The woman shrugged. "A new process. Do you care to try? Fifty yen to lose one kilo of body fat."

Trinja and I both burst into laughter. "And how long is it before the weight disappears?" she asked.

The woman never even cracked a smile. "Instantly. Body fat is gone instantly." She gestured to a small lever on the side nearest to her. "I regulate the power flow according to your payment."

My mouth dropped open. "But that's impossible! No exercise? No chemicals? No starving on a retreat week?"

"No." The woman folded her arms and leaned against the smooth white sides of her cubicle, as if she didn't much care whether we tried her new process or not. Trinja and I stared at each other. I was wondering if the woman had tried her machine herself—she didn't have one bit of fat.

"You got any money?" I asked Trinja. As she was shaking her head, I was rummaging through my pack. "I've got a hundred yen."

"Two kilos then," the woman said, taking my money with one hand and setting her lever with the other. She literally pushed me into the booth and the door slammed behind me.

At first I wanted to scream because I was so scared. The whole thing had happened too fast. I wanted to prove that this woman and her slimmer were a big joke, but suddenly I was trapped in a coffin-like structure as bare and as bright as an old microwave oven. My heart was hammering and the hair on the back of my neck stood up straight. I opened my mouth, but before I could scream there was a loud humming sound and instantly the door flew open again. I saw Trinja's frightened face peering in at me.

"Are you all right, Deb? Are you okay? I guess she decided not to do anything after all. You ought to get your money back."

"Two kilos are gone," the woman said in her strange voice.

Trinja pulled me away. "I'll just bet!" she shouted back at the woman. "Somebody ought to report you and that phony machine! We might even call the Health Brigade Corp!" She leaned closer to me. "Are you really okay, Deb?"

I took a deep breath. "My jeans feel loose."

Frowning, Trinja shook her head. "It's just your imagination, that's all. What a fake! The only thing slimmer after a treatment like that is your bank account. Nobody, but nobody, can lose weight that easily. We'll go to my house and you can weigh yourself. You haven't lost a gram."

But Trinja was wrong. I really was two kilos lighter. I know it sounds impossible, but Trinja's cal-show is never wrong. The two of us hopped and howled with joy. Then we ravaged her bedroom trying to find some more money. We ran all the way back to the mall, worrying all the way that the woman and her miracle machine might have disappeared. But the slimmer was still there. Within minutes Trinja had used up her three hundred yen, and she looked terrific.

"I can't believe it! I just can't believe it!" she kept saying as she notched her belt tighter. "Six kilos gone in seconds!"

"For safety's sake I'll have to prick your wrist, my dear," the woman said. "For every five kilos you lose we give a tiny little mark. Nobody will ever notice it."

"It didn't even hurt," Trinja said as we walked home. And neither of us could see the tiny blue pinprick unless we looked closely. We were both so happy about the weight loss that we almost floated. All our worries and problems about calories and fat and diets were over forever.

In no time at all the slimmers were all over the city, near all the swoodie stores. They've been a real blessing. Everybody says so. A few people have so many blue marks on their wrists that you can see them, but most have just four or five pinpricks.

← **Narrative Text Pattern**

Climax: Tension builds to the point where the character(s) succeed or fail at solving the problem. At this point the problem *seems* to be solved. Often, readers can't tell the true climax of a story until they reach the end. As you continue to read, think about whether this point in the story represents the climax.

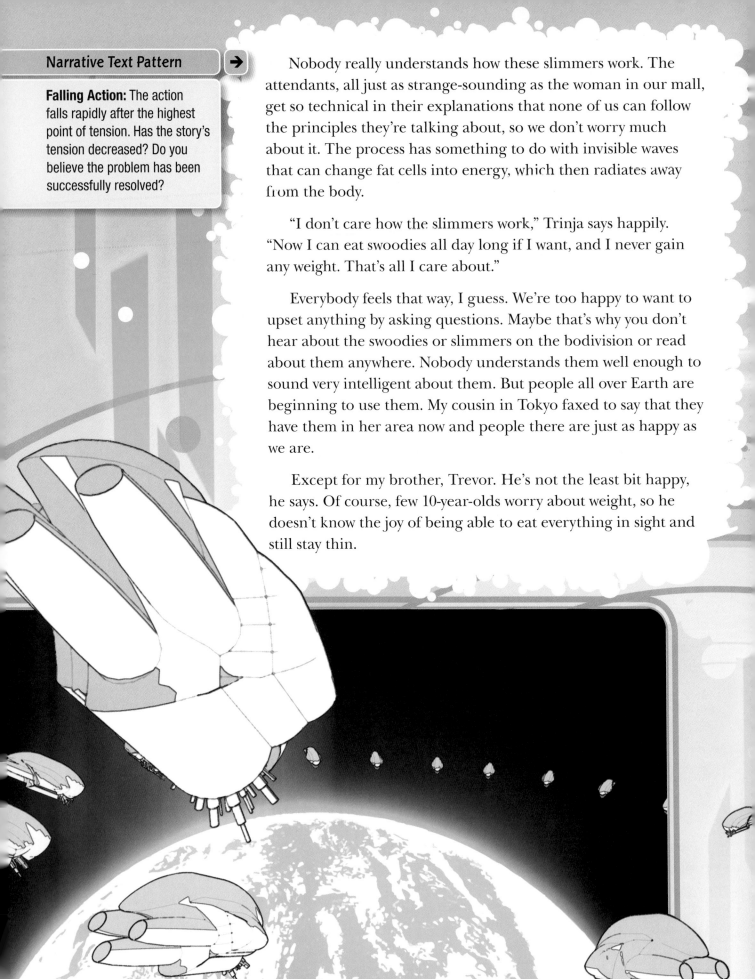

Narrative Text Pattern →

Falling Action: The action falls rapidly after the highest point of tension. Has the story's tension decreased? Do you believe the problem has been successfully resolved?

Nobody really understands how these slimmers work. The attendants, all just as strange-sounding as the woman in our mall, get so technical in their explanations that none of us can follow the principles they're talking about, so we don't worry much about it. The process has something to do with invisible waves that can change fat cells into energy, which then radiates away from the body.

"I don't care how the slimmers work," Trinja says happily. "Now I can eat swoodies all day long if I want, and I never gain any weight. That's all I care about."

Everybody feels that way, I guess. We're too happy to want to upset anything by asking questions. Maybe that's why you don't hear about the swoodies or slimmers on the bodivision or read about them anywhere. Nobody understands them well enough to sound very intelligent about them. But people all over Earth are beginning to use them. My cousin in Tokyo faxed to say that they have them in her area now and people there are just as happy as we are.

Except for my brother, Trevor. He's not the least bit happy, he says. Of course, few 10-year-olds worry about weight, so he doesn't know the joy of being able to eat everything in sight and still stay thin.

"Suppose the swoodies and the slimmers are run by aliens from outer space," he says. "From lots farther than we've been able to go. Maybe they have big starships posted around Earth, and they're gathering up the energy from human fat that's sent up from the slimmers. Maybe the swoodies are here so people will get fat quicker so that there'll be more to harvest through the slimmer machines. Then they'll take the fat back to their planet and use it as fuel."

"That's the dumbest thing I've ever heard of!" Trinja tells him. "Why don't we hear about the spaceships, then? Why doesn't the Health Brigade Corp tell us to stop doing this if it isn't good for us?"

Trevor thinks he has the answers. He says the spaceships are invisible to human detection, and he says the aliens have hypnotized our leaders into being as calm and placid as we all are. The blue marks on our wrists play a big role. He says maybe after each of us has had so many blue marks, we'll be culled from the flock because our fat content won't be as good any more.

He's crazy, isn't he? He must think we all have the brains of sheep. Ten-year-old brothers can be a real pain. He simply doesn't know people yet, that's all. Humans would never sacrifice their freedom and dignity just so they could eat and still be thin. Even aliens ought to know that.

I could quit eating swoodies and using those slimmers any time I want to.

But all those little blue marks Trinja and I have are beginning to look like delicate tattooed bracelets, and we both think they look really neat on our wrists.

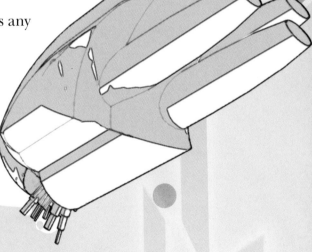

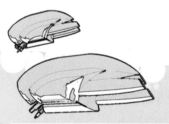

Narrative Text Pattern

Resolution: The falling action leads to the ending, or resolution, of the story. Many stories include a surprise ending. Would you consider the ending of this story a surprise? What clues throughout the story helped you predict this ending?

Reflecting

Understanding Text Patterns: How effectively does the author, Carol Farley, use the narrative elements and pattern? How would you change the story if you could?

Metacognition: At what point in the story did you realize that there was going to be a surprise ending? What inferences did you make that helped you determine that?

Critical Literacy: In narrative, perspective—or point of view—is provided by the narrator. How would this story be different if Trevor were narrating instead of Deb?

Talk About It
What do you predict will be the theme of "The Final Program"?

The Final Program

Short Story by Stephen Bowkett

Surfer made the stars green that night, the sky lilac, and the full moon a wonderful amber yellow. The others couldn't really complain, because they did crazy things sometimes—and it was Surfer's thirteenth birthday.

The rest of the group, Rom, Qwerty, and Byte, sang "Happy Birthday" tunelessly, then created the New Millennium World Choir to do the job properly. Surfer was suitably impressed and shared out his cake.

Afterward they threw the pieces they couldn't eat to a flock of circling dragons made entirely of glass.

"I suppose we'd better get on with the homework," Qwerty said at last. She was the only girl in the group, and the most practical. She wore her real face whenever the four of them met. And it was a friendly face, framed by long dark hair and lit by cheerful blue eyes.

At least, Qwerty said it was her real face, and the boys saw no reason to doubt her.

They all lived in different parts of the city and got together twice a week in Virtual Reality dataspace to help each other with their studies. Rom was the real genius with computers, and while the others struggled over their assignments, he created figures in the air—endless zeroes and ones of binary code—out of which he created new programs. Last week he'd made the glass dragons; this week's task was to form an entire army of crystal dinosaurs.

Rom also loved to explore, surfing the VR Internet for interesting new websites. As the others watched an electric motor taking itself to pieces in the sky, while a chatty voice explained how it worked, Rom disappeared into the distance.

Once the electric motor was completely dismantled, the teacher's voice told the children how it was different from gas engines and jet engines. Then all the pieces rushed together; the motor started spinning and zoomed away into the heavens.

"Next week," the teacher told them, "we'll look at rocket engines!"

"Great," Surfer yawned, then frowned. "Imagine having to do homework on my birthday!"

There was a flash of silver lightning across the starry heavens and Rom reappeared. The others jumped with shock.

"You scared me half to death!" Surfer complained. He stepped away as Rom's body rippled and quivered. Rom shrank fifteen centimetres as he became a thirteen-year-old boy with a mass of reddish hair and a face peppered with freckles.

"Is that what you really look like?" Byte wondered.

Qwerty grinned. "I think he's cute."

Rom ignored their comments. "You'll never guess what I found—"

"A genie in a bottle," was Surfer's sarcastic guess.

Rom jabbed a finger at him. "Something just as good … It's a website: a very special website, one created by Professor Todd Michaelson."

"Who's he?" Surfer wanted to know.

"Only the most brilliant VR engineer of all time. He hasn't been heard of for a few years now, and the word among the Webheads is that the World Government has hidden him away so he can work on his Theory of Holomorphic Projection."

Surfer gave Rom a puzzled look. "What's that mean?"

"It's a way of creating Virtual Reality without the headset and datasuit," Rom replied. "A way of projecting computer images into the real world, so you'll never know the difference."

Surfer gave a mocking laugh. But then he went quiet, because Rom wasn't laughing at all, and Qwerty herself actually looked a little frightened.

"We shouldn't have anything to do with it," she warned.

Rom screwed up his face in disagreement. "Get real! Ever since the Internet came into existence, people have been hacking into its secret corners … I mean, if you came to a wonderful old forest with a Keep Out sign, what would you do?"

"Go in," Surfer giggled mischievously. Byte nodded agreement.

"Me too." Rom gazed at Qwerty challengingly.

"I'd stay away," she said, "because if there wasn't any danger, there wouldn't be a fence…."

In the world of the Web, fences were made out of cryptic codes and electronic warnings that flashed across the sky. It took no time at all for the four friends to get to Professor Michaelson's website— just a short leap of the imagination.

"Of course," Rom said airily, "if the rumours about him were true, then there's always the chance that Michaelson wanted someone to find this way in. Perhaps he wasn't happy to be smuggled away by the Government."

They were standing in a place on the very edge of nowhere. The sky was filled with a storm of light and shadows, out of which tumbled sounds like cracked church bells in a ruined tower. Just ahead of them was something that looked like a wall, running with slime and hung with grey cobwebs.

"Nobody's bothered to fill in the details of the site," Rom pointed out. "It's just a forgotten corner on the Net. But look—"

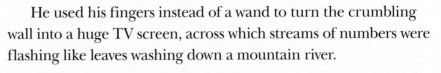

He used his fingers instead of a wand to turn the crumbling wall into a huge TV screen, across which streams of numbers were flashing like leaves washing down a mountain river.

The light began to change and the ground flowed like mist around them—rising upward, then swirling away to show a fine old house with lots of trees in the grounds and a view of the city spread out before them in the cup of the valley.

"Hey," Byte exclaimed. "I know this place! It's Westridge. My aunt and uncle live up here."

"I guess this must be Michaelson's house." Rom took a few steps forward, then looked at the others, who were hanging back. "What's the problem?"

"Sometimes," Qwerty answered in a small voice, "if the Keep Out sign doesn't work, people use guard dogs…."

Rom tutted with irritation, but he backtracked to where his friends were standing.

"Look, we have three alternatives. We just walk away and go back to that *boring* homework. Or we can try to decipher the data-locks here in VR and see what Michaelson's up to."

"Or?" Qwerty propped her hands on her hips, noting the gleam in Rom's eye.

"Or we go to Westridge *in the flesh.*"

"That's an ace idea," Surfer said, his face lighting up. "I mean, we've never actually met each other, have we—not, like, in person? I'm in," Surfer said, and held out his hand. Byte placed his own hand above it, and Rom laid his over that. Qwerty hesitated, then shrugged and rested her hand on top.

"Tomorrow," she decided for them. "After classes."

The others nodded as if they thought this was the beginning of a great adventure, but Qwerty wondered what the point was. After all, the flesh beneath her palm was warm and smooth and alive—as real as she could ever want it to be.

Qwerty's parents would only let her travel to another part of the city the next day on the condition that she took her personal monitor—and promised to be back no later than eight o'clock. It was early October and would be getting dark by then.

"It's never dark in the city," Qwerty pointed out with a chuckle. "Everything carries on just as usual, twenty-four hours a day."

Qwerty's mother gave a patient sigh, and not just because her daughter was challenging what she said.

"You know, when I was a young girl, Mom and Dad used to take us kids out into the country. Dad had a small telescope that he used to set up on the tripod, and we'd sit by the car and have a picnic until the sun went down and the stars came out. And then we'd look for any planets visible in the sky that night— Venus, Mars, Jupiter—and they were all different colours … and we'd have competitions to name as many craters on the moon as we could … and finally, we'd find the misty arc of the Milky Way. Why, I don't think you've ever *seen* the Milky Way!"

"We did a project on space last term," Qwerty said casually. "And I went to the centre of the Galaxy in a hyperlight ship to see what it was like."

Qwerty's mother jabbed a finger at her daughter's computer terminal as a sudden anger clouded her face. "No you didn't, because that was an illusion. The truth isn't in there." She looked at the VR headset and the shimmery pile of cellophane-like material that Qwerty wore to immerse herself in dataspace. "It's out in the real world. You would do well to remember that, Eleanor. Living a life of dreams all the time just isn't healthy, my girl."

Qwerty apologized and made a pot of tea to prove it. But even after they were friends again she had a strange feeling inside, which she didn't understand until she was halfway across the city, travelling by subway to Westridge…. Her mother had called her Eleanor, which was her real name, but she'd been Qwerty for so long, to so many people, that she felt completely at ease with it now—so much so that Eleanor sounded like a name that belonged to a stranger.

The subway ended about a kilometre from Michaelson's house, and of course the autotaxis only operated within the city centre. Qwerty realized she'd have to walk, which seemed like a real chore at first—because in the Web you could go anywhere in no time at all—but once she got into her stride, she quite enjoyed herself.

Her journey was uneventful, except that her mother called her on the monitor to ask what she was doing way over at Westridge. Her face on the tiny TV screen looked concerned.

"It's Rom's idea, Mom," Qwerty explained. "There's a Webhead up here who's a wizard at writing VR programs. We thought we'd pay him a visit. An interview would make a great chapter for my next InfoTech assignment!"

"Well, I can't argue with that. But take care!"

"Of course I will. And if it'll make you feel any better, I'll take an autotaxi back home … as long as you pay for it."

Qwerty's mother grinned. "All right, you win. Charge it to my CredCard. See you later, Eleanor."

"Bye Mom," Qwerty said, as the holographic image faded. Five minutes later she spotted Surfer standing by the gates of a large house she recognized as Michaelson's. At least, she assumed it was Surfer. But this boy wore glasses, and as he waved and smiled in greeting, Qwerty saw that he had metal braces.

"Wow," Surfer said, "you're even prettier in real life!"

"Um, thanks." Qwerty wasn't sure how to respond to the compliment. I can't return it, that's for sure, she thought.

Surfer must have read her eyes, because his face clouded and he shrugged.

"Yeah, Qwerty, it's sad—but most kids I know change how they look when they do VR."

Qwerty totally surprised Surfer by giving him a friendly hug. "Do you realize this is the first time we've met in real life? I prefer you just as you are. You always seem so arrogant in the Web."

Surfer grinned. "Part of the image. But thanks for making me feel better."

"No problem," Qwerty said. "And while we're out here, call me Eleanor, okay?"

"Deal," said Surfer, blushing slightly. "I'm Gavin."

He explained that Rom and Byte had asked him to look out for her, while they went inside to talk with Professor Michaelson. "You mean Michaelson is alive? And he's here?"

"It looks like Rom was making a big fuss out of nothing. Michaelson himself answered the door. Rom explained we were datafreaks, and could we do an interview. Michaelson seemed really pleased to see us."

They walked toward the front door, which had been left ajar for them, and went into the house, passing an elderly lady who was carrying a tea tray in the hall, then walking through to the study where the others were gathered.

Professor Michaelson greeted Qwerty warmly as Rom introduced her.

"But please, call me Eleanor," she insisted.

"A young lady who knows her own mind. That'll be useful later on," Michaelson said, smiling. But it was, to Eleanor's eyes, a rather vague smile, as though the man's mind was absorbed with other, darker thoughts.

"We were surprised to find you here," Rom said.

"I—uh—I chose to be here," Michaelson confessed. "When you found my Website and broke the codes to enter, I knew you would be the ones to carry on my work."

Rom's mouth dropped open. "You mean—you want us—me—to help you with your Holomorphic Projection Theory?" His eyes flicked again to the terminal in the corner.

Michaelson followed his gaze. "You'll be using terminals like that one, and I hope machines a million times more powerful. There is much work to be done, and I think your friends will be very precious to you in the weeks and months to come."

"I don't understand, sir—"

"There is little time, so I must explain quickly," Michaelson said.

Eleanor found she had to strain to see him, for the room was becoming gloomier, and now a thread of lightning flickered across the sky, followed by a distant soft boom of thunder.

The professor rose and moved towards the patio doors that led out into a private garden bordered with tall trees. As he opened the doors, they were flung back by a gust of wind.

"The weather's getting worse," Byte yelled.

"Ah, young man, don't worry yourself. They won't risk interfering too much—yet!"

"What do you mean, professor?" Eleanor found she had to shout over the rush and roar of the approaching storm. "Who are 'they'?"

Michaelson leaned close to her. His face was very intense. "When my wife was alive, she loved embroidery and would spend hours weaving an intricate picture—a landscape, a face. Sometimes she found a mistake and would always unpick the stitches to put it right. Always, no matter how much of the picture she was forced to unravel."

"I'm sorry," Eleanor told him. "I thought that was your wife I saw in the hallway."

"Oh," Michaelson said, "it was … but I see you still don't understand. This way—come quickly now!"

He hustled the children through the garden to a spot hidden by trees and thick beech hedges. Here the wind was muted, and the black clouds overhead streamed harmlessly by.

Eleanor found herself looking at two marble headstones, and felt her chest tightening with horror or amazement or both as she read their gilded inscriptions.

Emily Sarah Michaelson, born 1953, died 2029. Rest in Peace.

"But they won't let her rest!" Michaelson suddenly snarled, shaking his fist at the sky. "And I won't let them rest because of it! Do you hear me? You shall not have this power!"

Thunder answered and the whole city shuddered.

Eleanor grabbed at Michaelson's arm, just to make sure it was real. It seemed as solid as her own flesh, and she shook her head in confusion.

"Professor, what's going on here? That other gravestone—it's yours! You're buried there!"

Michaelson laughed at the children's bewilderment. "Am I a man dreaming he's a butterfly—or a butterfly dreaming he's a man? I don't know. But we must all be allowed to dream what we choose. Don't you agree? Wouldn't you fight for the right to do that?"

Rom pushed his way forward and stood before Michaelson. He looked fearful, but determined. "You need to show me how to work the terminal, professor." He glanced at the others. "If they want to help me, fine. But one of us has got to stay here to break the codes of the final program."

"Yes!" Michaelson grabbed Rom's hands and shook them with a desperate gratitude. "Bless you, boy. I'll show you now. Let's get back."

Without knowing why, Eleanor found herself hurrying with the others towards the house. Her pulse was racing and a terrible apprehension had gripped her heart. Something awful was going on: Michaelson had discovered what it was long ago, it appeared—and now Rom also understood…. They burst into the study an instant ahead of a vast thunderclap that rocked the house. Michaelson stumbled and clutched at his chest with a groan, but helped by the children, he reached the VR terminal.

"When you break through, you might find the world is a very different place," Michaelson said solemnly. "What are we like? What have we done to the earth to make all this necessary?"

"Professor, you've got to tell us—" Eleanor began, then screamed as Michaelson leaped up and staggered backwards with a yell.

The man's body was unravelling—tumbling apart into a million threads, and each thread breaking into a million coloured pixels, which faded away like dying sparks in the night.

Rom was hunched over the terminal, typing madly into the machine. "I've got to create new codes," he muttered, as though to himself. "Mustn't let them in…."

"Who, Rom, who?" Eleanor shouted, shaking him.

Rom turned to her and with a terrible look on his face said, "The people who made this dream!"

Then he spun back to his work and would say no more. Eleanor stumbled back, realizing at last. She looked for Byte and Surfer, but there was no sign of them, and now that didn't surprise her at all. She wondered how many others were just phantoms in the mind of the cosmic computer; ideas in the embroidery of the world?

And am I? Eleanor thought, as she went to the window and gazed out. Far away, the sun was dissolving like a lump of chalk in a watery sky. The hills were collapsing to dust, and the dust fading to nothing. Along every street, the lights were going out as the city crumbled back to raw data.

Am I a butterfly dreaming she's a girl? Eleanor asked herself, or a girl dreaming—

Reflecting

Understanding Text Patterns: What was the problem or conflict in this story? How was it resolved?

Metacognition: How does your understanding of Internet communication help you understand the major theme of this story?

Critical Thinking: How well does the title connect to the story? What do you now think is the theme of "The Final Program"?

The reading strategy you learned in this unit can help you to better understand text in other subject areas. Think about the questions you would ask yourself as you read this mathematics text.

Avoiding Bias in Data Collection

Goal – Understand different ways to collect data and analyze bias in data-collection methods.

Learn about the Math

At Fleury Public School, many students seem to arrive for class late. The student council has proposed starting school 1 h later. Ms. Chan, the student council adviser, wants the council members to gather some data to support their proposal.

The council members start by brainstorming ways to gather the data they need.

Peter: I think we should try an experiment. Half the school could start at the regular time, and the other half could start 1 h later. We could see if there are fewer students in the second group who are late for school.

Jasleen: We should do some research. If we find other schools that have a later start than us, we can ask them what the good and bad points are.

Ms. Chan: But what works for another school may not work here.

Heather: Let's survey all the students in Grade 7 to find out their opinions. We could use actual quotes to support our proposal.

Zach: Why don't we take a census? We could make a questionnaire and give it to every student in the school.

Ms. Chan: I think most students will want to start later, but I'm not sure if their parents or teachers will. We will have to get these opinions, too.

A survey may be biased in favour of or against different parts of a population. For each situation below, describe the groups for which the survey is likely to show bias.

Situation	Group that survey is likely biased in favour of	Group that survey is likely biased against
A company selects every 100th name in the phone book to call between 10:00 a.m. and 2:00 p.m., and doesn't leave messages. The question is "How many teenagers live in your home?"		
Every 10th person who walks by a particular intersection in downtown Toronto is asked, "Should hunting be banned in Ontario?"		
Every third person who enters a large toy store is asked, "Should the old age pension be increased?"		
On Saturday mornings, from 9:00 a.m. to 11:00 a.m., every 10th family entering the local zoo is asked, "How much time, on average, do you spend with your children?"		
An Internet survey is conducted to find out about computer use in Canadian households.		

biased results: when the results of a survey of one group are not likely to apply to another group selected from the same population

sample: a part of the population that is used to make predictions about the whole population

population: the total number of individuals or items

census: the counting of an entire population

Avoiding Bias in Data Collection

Digital divide in schools

Student access to and use of computers

Article from Statistics Canada

Schools appear to play a vital role in bridging a "digital divide" between rural and urban high school students. That's according to one of the first research papers done under the new Data Research Centre program. It looked at access to computers and the frequency of their use.

However, the same is apparently not the case when it comes to two other forms of digital divide: the gap between male and female students, and the gap between students whose parents have low levels of education and those whose parents are highly educated. Female students, in particular, tend to report lower levels of computer skills competency.

The vast majority of urban and rural youth, around 96% in both cases, reported using a computer during the 12 months prior to the 2000 General Social Survey, which collected information on the use of technology.

However, the study showed that high school students who live in rural areas are less likely to have a computer in their home than their counterparts in urban areas.

Data from the Youth in Transition Survey showed that only 8% of households with students aged 15 and 16 in cities with a population of 100 000 or more had no computer at home. However, the proportion was twice as high, around 18%, among students in villages with a population of less than 3000.

In contrast, 29% of students who lived in rural villages reported that they used a computer at school almost every day, compared with 19% of students in cities. In addition, 8% of rural youth reported almost daily computer use at libraries, compared with 4% of students in cities.

Reflecting

Metacognition: What kinds of questions do you ask most often when reading fiction? What kinds of questions do you ask most often when reading math text? What does this tell you about your thinking when you read these two kinds of text?

Critical Literacy: Why is it important for consumers to understand about bias in data collection when they see or hear ads that use survey data to sell a product?

Selections Grouped by Theme and Form

Index

Credits

Text

3–9 © 1975 Robert Zacks. 10–11 Buffy Saint-Marie © Caleb Music-ASCAP. 12–15 Adapted from HITLER YOUTH: GROWING UP IN HITLER'S SHADOW by Susan Campbell Bartoletti. Copyright © 2005 by Susan Campbell Bartoletti. Reprinted by permission of Scholastic Inc. 19–20 "Principals and Principles" first appeared in GUYS WRITE, GUYS READ (Viking, 2006). Permission for usage granted by the Charlotte Sheedy Literary Agency on behalf of Daniel Handler. 21–24 Permission for "Igniting Global Change, One Candle at a Time" granted by Free the Children. 25–29 Text from *If the World Were a Village* by David J. Smith and illustrations by Shelagh Armstrong used by permission of Kids Can Press Ltd., Toronto, Canada. Text © 2002 David J. Smith. Illustrations © 2002 Shelagh Armstrong. 31–33 © Simon Parke. 34-35 From FURTHER FABLES FOR OUR TIME Copyright © 1956 James Thurber, © renewed 1984 by Rosemary A. Thurber. Reprinted by arrangement with Rosemary A. Thurber and The Barbara Hogenson Agency, Inc. 36 Cover of *That Thing You Fall Into* © Diana Tamblyn: www.speedlines.com. Cover of *I.D.* by Vicki Grant, published by Orca Book Publishers, Victoria, B.C. 37 IDEAS printed with permission—Torstar Syndication Services. Cover of *Private Peaceful* © 2003 Michael Morpurgo. Mother Goose and Grimm © GRIMMY INC., KING FEATURES SYNDICATE. 40–41Written by Melissa Etheridge © 2006 Songs of Ridge Road (ASCAP). Used by permission. All rights reserved. 46–53 Taken from *The Birdman* © 2006 text by Veronika Martenova Charles, illustrations by Annouchka Gravel Galouchko and Stéphan Daigle originally published by Tundra Books. 59-62 From *Science on the Edge—Virtual Reality* 1ˢᵗ Edition by Tesar, Jenny (Author) 2003. Reprinted with permission of Gale, a division of Thomson Learning: www.thomsonrights.com. Fax 800 730-2215. 66–67 York Region Media Group. Reprinted with permission. 68–69 Used with permission from BBC News Online. 71–75 CNET.com, October 24, 2007. Reprinted with permission. 78–81 From *Cool Stuff and How it Works,* by Chris Woodford, Luke Collins, Clint Witchalls, Ben Morgan and James Flint. DK Publishing, Inc. New York, 2005. 95–103 © Carol Farley. 104–113 Used with permission from Steve Bowkett.

Photos

Cover: Protestors: Pascal Le Segretain/Getty Images. Sylvia Nowik/Shutterstock.

1 Masano Kawana/Getty Images. 2 © Jupiter Images, 2007. 10–11 Irene Teesalu/Shutterstock Background: Constant/Shutterstock. 10 Anastasios Kandris/Shutterstock. 11 War Poster Collection, Rare Books and Special Collections Division, McGill University Library. 12 © Karl Schnibbe. 13 © Karl Schnibbe. 14 © Karl Schnibbe. 15 © 2Sevens Media.16 People with globe: Vectro/Shutterstock; Tree: Noah Samson/Shutterstock. Penguins: BioWorkZ/Shutterstock. Dark globe: Michael D. Brown/Shutterstock. 17 Sillouettes: Kuzma/Shutterstock. Light globe: Maksim Samasiuk/Shutterstock. Tractor: Bjorn Heller/Shutterstock. Cityscape: Albert Campbell/Shutterstock. 19–20 Background: © Jupiter Images, 2007. 20 Sylvia Nowik/Shutterstock. 21 Courtesy Free the Children, www.freethechildren.ca. 22 Background: Masano Kawana/Getty Images; © Marie Abbott; © Dan Toolgood/Vancouver Courier. 25 Background: Natalia Siverina/Shutterstock; © Jupiter Images, 2007. 26 Background to pie chart: Janfilip/Shutterstock; © Jupiter Images, 2007. 27 © Jupiter Images, 2007. 28 Jupiter Images, 2007. 29 Water drops: Marc Chinotti/Shutterstock; © Jupiter Images, 2007. 30 © Tim Pannell/Corbis. 38-39 ZITS PARTNERSHIP, KING FEATURES SYNDICATE. 40–41 Background: Natalia Siverina/Shutterstock. 42 Photocreate/Shutterstock. 54 © Dale Wilson/Masterfile. 55 (t) U.S. Department of Energy. © Photolink/Getty Images. 56 D. Falconer/Photolink/Getty Images. 57 TheSupe87/shutterstock (background). Sean Gladwell/shutterstock (background). Jaime Duplass/shutterstock